Beginner's
Spinning

CH00677345

Beginner's Guides are available on the following subjects

Audio
Building Construction
Cameras
Central Heating
Colour Television
Computers
Digital Electronics
Domestic Plumbing
Electric Wiring
Electronics
Fabric Dyeing and Printing
Gemmology
Home Energy Saving
Integrated Circuits
Microprocessors
Photography
Processing and Printing
Radio
Spinning
Super-8 Film Making
Tape Recording
Technical Illustration
Television
Transistors
Video
Weaving
Woodturning
Woodworking

Beginner's Guide to
Spinning

Hetty M. Wickens

Newnes Technical Books

Newnes Technical Books

is an imprint of the Butterworth Group

which has principal offices in

London, Boston, Durban, Singapore, Sydney, Toronto, Wellington

First published 1982

British Library Cataloguing in Publication Data
Wickens, Hetty M.
  Beginner's guide to spinning.
  1. Hand spinning
  I. Title
  746.1'2   TT847

  ISBN 0-408-00573-4

Photoset by Butterworths Litho Preparation Department
Printed in England by Whitstable Litho Ltd, Whitstable, Kent

Preface

This book tries to show that a knowledge of spinning can be very useful, can enrich one's life, and can give great pleasure. Wool is discussed at greatest length because woollen fibres are fairly easily obtained and they are not difficult to spin. Having learned to use wool, one can apply this knowledge to many other fibres.

The book has two approaches. On the one hand, it outlines knowledge and techniques which have been handed down to us over many generations, and on the other, it is intended to encourage inventiveness, creative ideas, adventure, and exploration. A speaker at a textile society meeting once said, 'They didn't know it was impossible, so they got busy and did it'. So do not let techniques be your master: become competent, and then if you do not know a suitable technique, perhaps you can invent one.

Textile manufacture has become a scientific industry. Knowledge and skill have increased, yet mass production and financial restraints have led to restricted choice. So it is good to know that, when deciding to spin, we can be in charge of the situation: we are responsible for developing an idea through every stage until it reaches the finished article. Those who wish to add to their textile skills may like to know of the *Beginner's Guides* to weaving and to dyeing and printing in this series.

E. W.

Contents

With Compliments

KM Photography

Commercial & Industrial Photographic Services

257 **BREDON AVENUE**
BINLEY
COVENTRY CV3 2FD
Telephone: (0203) 450873

1

Wool and sheep

Wool

Wool from sheep is one of the easiest and most rewarding
fibres to learn to spin.

There are many different breeds of sheep in the British
Isles, as well as crossbreds and halfbreds. It is necessary to
find the sheep which provides the right type of wool, and
then the right part of the fleece needs to be found.

The woollen fibre
Wool may be coarse or fine, lustrous or dull, crimped or
straight, long or short, soft or harsh, white or naturally
coloured. It varies according to the part of the body on which
it grows; climate, pasture, food, and health affect it too.

Wool grows in locks, which are called the 'staple', each
consisting of thousands of individual fibres. If a fibre is
examined under a microscope, scales can be seen overlapping each other from the root in the direction of the tip. The
wool is lustrous when the scales are large and flat; long-
stapled wool usually has large scales, so length and lustre go
together. When the scales are small and projecting, as in
many fine, short-stapled wools, the surface is dull. Woollen
cloths can be given a proper finish because the scaly construction encourages felting.

Fibres are crimped from side to side and along the length. This enables wool to trap air and accounts for its great resilience. (A Merino fibre could have 30 crimps per inch.)

There is a small oil-gland at the base of each fibre which lubricates it during growth. This natural oil helps the hand-spinner if the wool is spun before washing ('in the grease'). When wool is dry, it often needs olive oil or something similar to be added to it before spinning.

Quality numbers and yarn count

There is a scale of numbers which has been handed down through generations to describe the fineness of fibre. These numbers are learned by experience and handling of wools. The scale starts at 28 and ends at 100 (the finest quality). Scottish Blackface wool can be described as having a quality number of 28, and merino could, rarely, be described as having a quality number of 100.

The number 28 means that 28 skeins of singles could be spun from 1 lb of wool. A skein is 560 yd, so 1 lb of 28s wool could produce 28 × 560 yd = 15,680 yd of singles. (In fact, a spinner would probably spin a thicker thread, so fewer yards would be spun from the pound.) 100s means that 100 skeins of singles could be spun from 1 lb of wool (in theory), and so on. The length of the skein remains constant, but fibres do not all have the same constant, and in the case of wool, each spinning method has its own constant. Moreover, the skein is called by different names for different fibres (e.g., hanks, leas, cuts).

If a singles yarn has been plied, a figure is written before or after the singles size to describe the number of singles used: e.g., if 10s woollen had been made into two-ply, it would be written 2/10s or 10s/2, meaning that 10 skeins of singles had been made into two-ply, giving five skeins of two-ply.

Yarn constants or standards are as follows.

Worsted	– 560 yd in a skein
Woollen	– 256 yd in a skein (Yorkshire woollen count)
Cotton	– 840 yd in a hank

Linen	– 300 yd in a lea
Tweed	– 200 yd in a cut
Spun silk	– 840 yd in a skein

The term 'denier' means the weight in grams of 9000 metres. In another international system, the 'tex', the count of yarn is the weight in grams of one kilometre of yarn.

Staple and kemp
The words 'staple' and 'kemp' often occur when discussing wool.

Staple describes the length of the woollen fibres, so there are short-stapled, medium-stapled, and long-stapled wools.

Kemps are short, thick, wavy fibres with a pointed tip and root. They are shed periodically into the fleece. They have a white, chalky appearance, as they have a wide, central air canal (medulla). As a result, they do not dye, and they show up in material as dead-white hairs. They are very obvious in Harris tweed. Kemp occurs in mountain breeds of sheep, particularly in wet areas, where the kemp helps to shed the rain. Red and grey kemp can be found in Welsh mountain breeds.

Shrinkage
Shrinkage, which is mostly caused by the scaly surface and elasticity of wool, can take place by relaxation or by felting.

Relaxation shrinkage As wool is an elastic fibre, it will become stretched during spinning and weaving. While the fibre is dry, it will not shrink, as it can stretch and return to its shape, but when wet it is softened and able to relax more.

Felting shrinkage This is unique to wool and other animal fibres. Felting takes place when wet wool is repeatedly compressed and then allowed to relax. The fabric becomes thick, the fibres are matted, and much of their elasticity is lost. The exact cause is not known, but the scaly surface is probably the most important factor.

Felting at the laundry Rubbing will cause felting in wool, and some indoor dryers which tumble damp fabrics during drying may encourage it. Some wools felt more easily than others, particularly those of the down breeds.

Advantages of felting   In the making of felt, no spinning or weaving is required. Shepherds' cloaks, tents, floor coverings, saddle covers, and bags can all be made from felt.

Woven material can be felted deliberately in finishing. In milling, for example, fabric is given a fluffy, matted texture, as is required for blankets.

Sheep

Sheep in the British Isles can be divided into three main groups according to the length of their wool. These groups are shortwool and down; mountain and hill; and longwool and lustre.

The groups are a rough guide to the areas where a sheep can be found, the quality numbers of its fleece, and to the length and weight of its wool.

The term 'crossbred' can be misleading. To some woolmen, it means any wool that is not Merino; it can be a descriptive word for a carpet wool; it can mean breeds resulting from crossing to obtain particular qualities. Biological and economic factors have combined to give us many flocks composed of crossbred sheep. As most purebred sheep are crossbred in origin, cross breeding was responsible for most sheep in the world.

Shortwool and down breeds

Southdown   The Southdown is the oldest of the down breeds, but its origin is obscure. It is native to the chalk hills around Lewes in East Sussex, but thrives on most good grassy pasture. Southdown sheep are to be found in southern England, the United States of America, parts of Europe, and New Zealand.

The Southdown sheep is small, hornless, and with short legs. It has a mouse-coloured face with upper parts and ears covered with short wool. Its wool is one of the finest in terms

4

of fibre diameter of all the British breeds; it is very soft and short with a close dense staple and very crimped. The fleece is white but it is liable to have occasional dark fibres. Experienced handspinners enjoy the softness, elasticity, and versatility of this wool, using it for such things as scarves, tweeds, and travelling rugs.

Hampshire Down   Hampshire Down sheep were established over 100 years ago in the area of Hampshire, Wiltshire Dorset and Berkshire. Southdown blood was introduced at some time. It is a large sheep with a dark face and dark legs and is hornless. Its fleece is compact.

Dorset Down   These sheep are found in Dorset, Hampshire, Somerset, New Zealand, Australia and Argentina. They are of a medium size with a greyish-brown face. The wool is highly valued because of its fine texture.

It is difficult to tell the difference between Hampshire and Dorset Downs. Hampshire Down wool is a little more open, and coloured soil can affect the colour of the wool.

Dorset Horn and Poll Dorset   Dorchester is a popular area for these sheep, and they do well in Australia. They have a white face and thin, symmetrically curved horns. It is of a very fine quality and one of the whitest of British wools. There are no grey or kempy fibres, and it has a lofty, crisp handle. These ewes can breed at any time of the year.

Suffolk Down   Norfolk Horn ewes were crossed with Southdown rams at the beginning of the 19th century to give the Suffolk Down, found all over the British Isles. The face and legs are black, with no wool on them. There is a tendency for dark fibres to be found in the fleece.

Oxford Down   These sheep are found in the Cotswolds, the Midlands, and overseas. Their face and legs are dark brown. It is one of the largest of the down breeds, with a heavy, open fleece of a good staple length. The Oxford Down was developed from a Cotswold × Hampshire with some Southdown blood. The long wool of the Cotswold has an effect on the staple length. It is very popular with handspinners.

5

These photographs show typical examples of sheep breeds as follows

(Opposite)
Southdown	Suffolk Down
Clun Forest	Scottish Blackface
Cheviot	Black Welsh
Lincoln	Romney Marsh

(This page)
Shetland	Jacob
Corriedale	Australian Merino

Shropshire Down   The Shropshire breed probably dates back to the 16th century. The sheep are hardy and of medium size; the face, ears, and legs are black. The fleece is dense, heavy, fine, and almost free from kemp or grey or black fibres. It is very pleasant to spin.

Clun Forest   The Clun Forest sheep lives chiefly on the hills round the borders of Shropshire and Powys and in lowland areas throughout England and Wales. It is hardy. The face is dark brown, with pricked ears and a forelock of white wool. The wool is dense in staple and of fine texture but liable to kemp and grey fibres. The quality of the fleece is uniform, so sorting is easy.

Ryland   The Ryland is said to be one of the oldest breeds in the country. The sheep, which are found on the vales and hillsides of Herefordshire, are compact and hornless. The wool has a soft, light handle, a delightful springiness, and a dense staple. There are practically no kemps or black or grey fibres. The resulting threads and cloths can have a smooth finish. This wool is resilient and has excellent elasticity. It is highly thought of throughout the world.

Kerry Hill   This sheep is native to the Kerry Hills in Powys, but there are registered flocks in 31 counties of England, Wales, Ireland, and the Isle of Man. The wool is white, crisp, and fairly fine. It is free from grey.

Devon Closewool   The Devon Closewool sheep is medium sized with a splendid fleece. It has been bred in North Devon for over 100 years.

Wiltshire Horn   A handspinner would not choose a Wiltshire Horn fleece. The breed has the distinction of producing very little wool, which is hairy and often matted. These sheep are kept solely for the purpose of producing rams for crossing.

Mountain breeds
Mountain and hill breeds, which are found on land over 1000 ft., usually have medium-length wool. It can be very harsh and coarse on the outside, but next to the body there is a soft undercoat. Kemp is usually found in these fleeces.

Cotswold   Cotswold sheep probably originated from sheep kept by the Romans on estates near Cirencester. They were reduced to a few flocks by the end of the 1914–1918 war, but the breed is now expanding. It is a big, hornless sheep with a white face and white legs. Its fleece is white, curly, and lustrous.

Scottish Blackface   This can be known as the Scottish Blackface, Mountain Blackface, or just Blackface. It lives on the high ground of northern England and Scotland and elsewhere and is thought to be a pure race. The sheep has a small body, spiral horns, a long shaggy coat, and a black face. It is extremely hardy. As well as being very coarse, the wool is open, harsh, and hairy. It is extremely popular with manufacturers of carpets and rugs. The hardwearing qualities, together with a natural springiness, enable the pile of carpet to resist tread marks and regain its position. Much of this wool is exported to Italy, where it is used for filling mattresses. A typical Blackface fleece can be divided into two kinds of coat: an outer coat of strong hairy fibres, and an inner, softer coat. Handspinners who want a coarse, strong, hardwearing thread for rugs or upholstery would find this very useful, as Blackface wool is in a class of its own.

Cheviot   This breed took its name from the range of hills running between England and Scotland. It is also found in Northumberland, South Wales, Canada, Scandinavia, the USA, South Africa, and New Zealand. They are of medium size with white face and legs. There is no wool on the face or on the legs below knee and hock, but there is a ruff of wool behind their ears. The staple is dense and the fibre sound, strong and crisp. Handspinners find this wool a very agreeable one to use and weavers appreciate its good milling properties.

Exmoor Horn   The Exmoor Horn is a hill breed which produces fine wool. Its fleece is compact, neat, clean, and attractive. The breed is found on the Devon and west Somerset hills and resembles the Dorset Horn.

Herdwick   The Herdwick is associated with the Lake District. Because it has been confined to a small area, some people claim it as the purest of all British breeds of sheep. It is small, agile and wiry. The carpet industry uses Herdwick wool, but the finer wool is used for woollens. Lambs are born almost black but the fleece becomes lighter with subsequent shearings. Because of its coarseness and variable colour, the wool is usually the cheapest of British wools. But when one requires a strong, hardwearing, resilient thread in natural colours, it is the ideal fleece. Locally manufactured 'hodden grey' was a coarse handwoven woollen cloth made from undyed yarns. This was very hardwearing and virtually waterproof.

Swaledale   The Swaledale is to be found in the northern counties of England on the Pennines. It is a very hardy, medium-sized sheep. The wool is coarse and very kempy, but the staple feels fine and soft near the body of the sheep. Finer-quality Swaledale fleeces may be used for tweeds, coarse knitting-wool, and rugwool, but on the whole it is particularly suited for carpets.

Welsh Mountain   This breed is small and active. The sheep are very hardy and thrive in wild, rough highlands as well as on lowlands. Kempy fibres are prevalent in the fleece; most kemp is white, but red or grey kemp can be found. The very best wool will be found to be fine, soft, and free of kemp and grey fibres. This will be suitable for shawls and flannels. The coarser wool is taken by the carpet trade.

Black Welsh   Flocks of this breed thrive in England, Scotland, Wales, and Ireland, and have excellent results when exported. Black Welsh wool is a great favourite with handspinners. The black, short, thick wool is firm to handle and does not require dyeing. This breed is also kept for ornamental purposes in parklands. The all-black fleece and denseness of wool look very attractive.

Masham   The Dalesbred was crossed with a Teeswater or Wensleydale to produce a Masham. The resulting fleece has a good, long staple and is practically impervious to rain and snow. Masham fleece, which is free from black, is very pleasant to use where a long, lustrous yarn is required. It is also very attractive when used in staple form; when the locks have been washed and combed, they make luxurious rugs, the fleece forming a pile from knots.

Longwool breeds

Sheep with long, lustrous wool are mainly found on the lowlands and coastal plains. This long wool was combed and spun into worsted threads in the Middle Ages.

Lincoln Longwool Lincoln Longwool sheep are descended from the original native sheep of the county. They are probably responsible for the foundation of all the lustre breeds in England. The Corriedale breed of New Zealand was developed from Lincoln × Merino. It is the largest and heaviest sheep in England and one of the largest in the world. It has a white face with a heavy forelock over the eyes. The legs are white and woolled. The wool is dense, lustrous, rather wavy, and very long in staple. Grey or kempy fibres are hardly ever found. The length of the staple can pose problems for a handspinner as some Lincoln wool is quite difficult to prepare, but the resulting fine, lustrous thread can be very rewarding.

Leicester It is thought that the original Leicester sheep were brought to this country by Flemish weavers in the reign of Edward III and that it was on their descendants that Robert Bakewell founded the Leicester. The Border Leicester and Wensleydale breeds were evolved from crosses between the improved Leicester and local breeds. They are very hardy animals and can be found in East Yorkshire, Durham, Lancashire, Cumbria, and in Australia and New Zealand. The breed is used for crossing with Swaledales, Blackface, and Suffolk. It is quite a large animal, hornless, with a white face, white legs and feet. The wool is long and wavy in staple, with a silky appearance; it is very even in length and in fibre diameter. There are no kempy or grey fibres.

Border Leicester This was bred towards the end of the 18th century from crosses between the Leicester and the Cheviot.

These sheep are found in northern England and the Scottish Lowlands, also in Australia, New Zealand, and South Africa. They are fairly big sheep, hornless with a white head, prominent ears and a Roman nose. The wool is lustrous, fairly open in staple, and not liable to kemp and grey fibres. Individual staples separate easily and end in a small curl. Handspinners will find it useful for worsted spinning and it will dye well. The crosses from a Border Leicester are important. Crossing with Cheviot produces the Halfbred; crossing with Blackface gives the Greyface.

Kent or Romney Marsh   Romneys are exported to many parts of the world, adapting to various climates and altitudes. It is the predominant breed in New Zealand. It is a hornless sheep with broad white face, and black nose and forelock. The wool is sound and fairly close in staple and it is fairly free from grey and kemp. The fleece is denser and finer than that of other British longwool breeds, less lustrous and with more crimp. The handspinner finds this fleece very useful for sleek, smooth threads.

Dartmoor   These sheep live in Devon and Cornwall on uncultivated moor and heath. Their long, lustrous, curly wool has good milling properties, and surfaces can be highly raised. It looks particularly attractive when dyed in strong, clear colours.

South Devon   South Devon sheep are found in south Devon, South Africa, and Argentina. The face is clean and the head is covered with curly wool. They are the biggest of the longwool breeds to be found in south-west England and one of the heaviest wool producers in the world. Even the lambs produce a heavy fleece. The wool has a long, fine staple; it is curly, lustrous, and dense.

Rare breeds

Soay   The small brown Soay is the last survivor or the prehistoric domestic sheep of Europe. They shed their coarse, hair-like wool in summer and are often not shorn but plucked. Because of their wild appearance and historic interest, they are often kept in zoos and private parks. They are very hardy and thrifty. Their wool can provide beautiful, soft threads in the hands of a patient, experienced spinner. Some of the wool is quite harsh and hairy, but the soft, short wool, while difficult to spin, is very rewarding.

Orkney   The Orkney represents the ancestral stock from which the modern Shetland breed developed. They feed almost entirely on seaweed, so the wool can be very sandy. They have multicoloured fleeces: the Wool Marketing Board makes five grades, which are white and near white; moorit (moor-red) and fawn; light grey; dark grey; and black and dark brown. There is a larger proportion of grey wool than black and moorit. The grey wool tends to be hairy, consisting of black, hairy fibres among white wool, but the wool can be as fine as the finest Shetland. There is a tendency to shed fleece, but the sheep are no longer plucked as they once were. These subtle colour changes and variations in texture enable discriminating handspinners to produce exquisite threads.

Manx Loghtan   The Loghtan is the native breed of the Isle of Man. It is a short-tailed sheep, often having four or six horns. The name is derived from the Manx words for mouse and brown, and it describes the colour. There is a flock of Loghtans on the Isle of Man kept by the Manx Museum, and a small flock at the Royal Showground, Stoneleigh. The wool is brown with fawn-gold tips. It is short-stapled and varies in quality from harsh to extremely soft.

St Kilda   The St Kilda sheep is a black or dark brown breed, now only found in private parks and zoos and on farms where there is a special interest in rare breeds. The black wool is of little commercial value, but handspinners and handweavers find it useful. Breeding or in-breeding affects the quality, which can vary from harsh to soft.

Shetland   The Shetland is one of the smallest British sheep. It is noted for the fineness and softness of its wool. This half-wild animal produces several shades of wool, including white, moorit, fawn, grey, and brown. Careful breeders keep different colours in separate flocks. The pure Shetland is in danger of becoming reduced in number because of crossing with Cheviots and Border Leicesters. The many knitted garments labelled 'Shetland' are not likely to have been made from this wool. It is a term used to describe 100% virgin wool spun on the woollen system, having the qualities which were attributed to products formerly made exclusively from Shetland Islands wool.

Jacob Jacob (or Spanish) sheep were a rare breed in Britain until the 1960s. There is a thriving Jacob Sheep Society which has encouraged many people to keep these sheep. Handspinners enjoy using Jacob wool because of its natural colours and variety of qualities within one fleece (see Chapter 12).

Other breeds

Merino The Merino is one of the earliest breeds of sheep. It is thought that the Carthaginians, who were among the earliest races to settle in Spain, took flocks with them.

In 1765, the Merino was sent to Saxony and the German breeders developed flocks with exceptionally fine wool. The fleece of a Saxony Merino is bright in colour and soft.

Louis XV allowed one of the largest estates of Rambouillet to be used for Merinos: it later became an experimental farm.

The breed was introduced into America in 1798, and the New England state of Vermont became a great sheep-breeding centre. It evolved the Vermont type of Merino, with a very wrinkly body.

The breed had become fairly well established in South Africa by 1804; at the beginning of the 19th century, some high-quality Merinos were imported from Australia to improve the flocks.

The first Merinos arrived in Australia in 1797. Great advances have been made in the breeding of the Merino, so types have been produced which suit the particular grazing and climatic conditions of such a large country.

The beautiful Merino fleece is not easy for beginners to spin, as the fibres are fine and greasy, but the thread when well-spun is beautifully soft. Quality numbers can start in the 60s and extend into the 90s.

Corriedale   The Corriedale gets its name from a property in New Zealand, where ewes of a British longwool breed were crossed with Merinos. In 1882, a stud of Corriedales was established in Australia, where they mated Lincoln ewes with Merino rams.

The fleece is heavy, even, and of good length. The wool is crimped and dense. It possesses good wearing qualities and has a soft handle. It is one of the most popular wools for handspinners.

Table 1.1. Sheep breeds

Breeds	Quality number	Staple length (in)	Fleece weight (lb)
Border Leicester	40–46	6–10	4–8
Cheviot	50–56	2–6	4–5
Clun Forest	56–58	3–4	5–7
Corriedale	50–56	4–6	9–12
Cotswold	40	12–14	15
Dalesbred	32–40	9	4
Dartmoor	34–38	9	14
Devon Closewool	46–50	5	8
Devon Longwool	32–36	12	16
Dorset Down	56–58	2–3	5–7
Dorset Horn	54–58	3–4	5–7
Exmoor Horn	48–52	3½–4½	6½–7½
Hampshire Down	50–58	2–3	4–5
Herdwick	32–40	5	4½
Jacob	48–56	4–5	5–6
Kent (Romney Marsh)	46–50	6–7	8½–10
Kerry Hill	48–56	4	4–7
Leicester	40–46	11–12	10–12
Lincoln Longwool	36–44	12–16	13–14
Masham	36–40	7–10	6
Merino	64–90	2–4	9–10
Orkney	50–56	1–3	2½
Oxford Down	50–58	6	8–10
Rough Fell	32–40	9–10	5
Ryeland	56–58	3–4	6–8
Scottish Blackface	28–32	8–13	4–7
Shetland	56–60	3–4	3
Shropshire	50–58	3½–4½	6–8
South Devon	36–40	12–16	18–21
Southdown	56–60	3½–4½	4½
Suffolk Down	56–58	2–3	6
Swaledale	28–32	8–12	3½–4
Teeswater	40–48	12	8
Welsh Mountain	32–50	3–4	2–2½
Welsh Black Mountain	46–54	3–4	4
Wensleydale	50	12	14

2

Sorting a fleece

Sorting is an extremely important part of the preparation of a fleece for spinning. It is a skill which takes a long time to learn, but beginners should be aware of the need to examine a fleece carefully, and with practice a knowledge of different types of wool will be developed.

Obtaining a fleece

Some wool can be collected from fences or hedges; it will probably be of poor quality, although it is better than nothing. In Britain, the British Wool Marketing Board has a special department which deals with handspinners' requests. The wool from rare breeds is of particular interest to handspinners, so if possible find out from a rare-breeds farm which merchant deals with their wool. Shops specialising in the sale of spinning and weaving equipment almost always have fleece for sale.

Shearing

It is helpful to consider how the fleece arrived at the state in which it is received.

After shearing, the wool falls to the floor. If the floor is clean, all is well; if not, there may be rubbish or string folded into the fleece.

Table 2.1. British wool fleeces available from the British Wool Marketing Board

Type No	Description	Average staple length (in)	Count	Handle	Colour	Approximate weight of normal greasy fleece (kg)
84226	Fine Wool White	3–4	56's	Soft	White	2–3
84291	Fine Wool Dark	3–4	56's	Soft	Grey/black	2–3
84308	Romney (Kent)	4–5	50–54's	Medium	White	3–4
84322	Leicester Cheviot Cross	6–7	50–54's	Soft/medium	White	3–4
84350	Jacob	5–6	50–56's	Soft	Piebald	1½–2
84413	Masham	4–6	46–48's	Medium/harsh	White	2–3
84491	Masham Dark	4–6	46–50's	Medium/harsh	Dark grey	2–3
84603	Cheviot	3–5	54–56's	Soft	White	2–3
84690	Welsh	2–3	48–56's	Soft/medium	Grey/black	1–2
84221	Fine Hogg Wool White	4–5	56's	Soft	White	2–3

A guide to use

Staple length

2 in staple – for the experienced spinner, suitable for woollen spinning

3 in–4 in staple – recommended for beginners, suitable for woollen spinning

5 in–7 in staple – recommended for beginners, suitable for worsted spinning

Over 7 in staple – better suited to the experienced spinner

Qualities

Soft to medium – suitable for spinning apparel fabrics

Medium to harsh – suitable for tweeds, coat and upholstery fabrics

Harsh – suitable for upholstery and floorcoverings

The fleece is folded into three before being tightly rolled.

The wool from the neck and head is pulled and twisted so that it looks like a tail. The neckbank contains very good wool – do not confuse it with the tail end of the sheep. (If sharing a fleece with someone, halve it down the middle from head to tail, for this will ensure a fair distribution of qualities.) The neckbank is taken round the tightly rolled fleece and tucked in. Sometimes baler twine is used; this causes the spinner many difficulties, so make sure all string is removed.

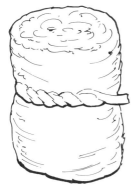

Figure 2.1.   A tightly rolled fleece

When huge numbers of sheep are being shorn, the neckband is not always twisted. The fleece is rapidly rolled up and tied with something like brown string (actually twisted brown paper, which is apparently less trouble to wool sorters because there are no loose fibres to get mixed into the fleece). This is not generally popular with the Wool Marketing Board.

Preparing to sort a fleece

A large space is needed, for a fleece will take up about four times the area of a sheepskin rug.

Spread newspaper or plastic sheeting on the floor, or on a fine day work outside.

Place cardboard boxes around the fleece so that they are ready to receive the different sorts (qualities or matchings). A felt-tip pen and sticky labels will also be required.

Opening the fleece

Open out the fleece, unrolling it carefully after freeing the neckband. Spread it out evenly on the floor, disturbing it as little as possible. The tips of the wool should be uppermost.

Examine the fleece to see if odds and ends have been tucked into the middle before it was rolled. Make sure that it was the neckband that was twisted; it is possible that the wool might have been rolled from the other end.

Examining the fleece

When the fleece has been spread out, the time has come to evaluate the wool.

Do not pull locks of wool out in a haphazard manner. If a lock needs closer examination, remove it carefully and put it back in the same place. When handling wool, use the hands rather than just the fingers; in this way, the staples can be parted easily.

The amount of best wool will vary, and every fleece will have its own distribution of qualities. Consider the following points when looking at a lock of wool: fineness, crimpiness, length, strength, lustre, handle (soft, harsh, or wiry), and colour.

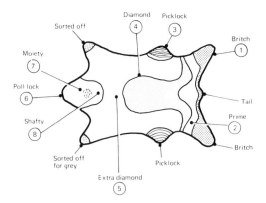

Figure 2.2. Traditional names for parts of the fleece

The illustrations give an indication of the areas where the divisions may be found. Different names are given to the wool; those used in *Figure 2.2* are traditional Sussex ones.

Skirting the fleece
Before separating the matchings, skirt the fleece: that is, pull off the dirty grey edges and, if the tail end is very dirty and soiled, place this wool in a bucket of water. The liquid will come in useful for fertilising the rose bushes.

Sorting

Look at *Figure 2.2* and start to separate the different grades.

1 Britch   Wool from the two hind legs, which is sometimes coarse and always coarser than the rest of the fleece. This wool is suitable for carpets, blankets and coarse materials.

2 Prime   Next to the britch, this wool is hollow, short, dusty, and of a frothy appearance. It is usually tender and should not be used where a strong wool is required, as it can lead to broken threads. Its tenderness can sometimes show during teasing, because the wool can pull apart between the fingers and break. If this happens, do not write off the whole fleece.

3 Picklock   Break off the wool which grows under the body of the sheep next. This wool is fine, short, flat, and without much staple. It can safely be used for fine work where the length of staple is not important, such as delicate weft threads.

4 Diamond   This is second-quality wool and it varies greatly in extent; a fleece may be all diamond. It joins the prime and runs up the hollow of the back. Compared with the best quality wool, it may be coarser, more open haired, and a little longer in staple, so it is a good section for beginners to use.

5 Extra diamond   This is the best quality wool, growing mostly on the flanks and shoulders. By selective breeding, this wool can be encouraged to take in nearly the whole fleece. Be prepared to find different amounts of this wool each time you are sorting. It is strong, dense, and of good staple. It can safely be used for the best work.

6 *Poll-lock* A roughish little lock of wool growing on the head. It can be thrown out for grey or placed with the diamond.

7 *Moiety* This small piece of wool grows on the neck. It consists of half wool and half chaff. Trough-fed sheep are liable to have hayseeds matted into their wool, so sort this out in order to avoid having vegetable matter in the spun threads and save time when teasing.

8 *Shafty* This is a long-stapled, strong, and useful wool, coarser than diamond. Finer fleeces do not have any shafty, but look for it towards the britch end of the fleece and a little behind the poll lock.

Paint and tar marks should be clipped off just below the surface in order to avoid any discolouration in the finished thread.

Below-average fleeces
In a below-average fleece, there may be no extra diamond, and shafty might be found in places usually occupied by diamond and prime.

It is helpful to keep notes concerning the types of wool found on individual fleeces.

Grey wool and kemp
Always be on the look-out for grey wool. In a white fleece, it can cause a great deal of trouble, and unfortunately it may not show up until the wool has been washed, dyed, and woven. Do not throw grey wool away, but use it where greyness does not matter, or dye it.

Kemp should be sorted out unless it is wanted for a particular effect.

The effects of bad sorting

The spun yarn could be uneven, because different parts of the fleece will give various results according to their elasticity and strength.

Dyeing will not be level if coarse and fine staples have been mixed.

If the wool is to be knitted, there could be problems with the tension. Shrinkage could happen, perhaps only in certain places, leaving the garment distorted.

In warp threads, if staples with differing crimps have been used, the tension will be uneven because of irregular elasticity.

The results of bad sorting may not show up until the woven or knitted cloth is being finished, when irregular felting qualities could spoil the whole effect.

But take heart: you may want some of those things to happen. You may want different rates of elasticity to get an undulating surface for a hanging. Uneven dyeing might meet your requirements exactly. Perhaps not a distorted garment, but a distorted wall hanging might be purposely planned.

Sorting for worsted spinning

Extra care is needed when sorting for worsted spinning. The staple should be 4 in or longer. Shorter staples can be combed, but the resulting thread will be a little whiskery and will not be sleek and lustrous. Some fleeces have an extremely long staple and can be difficult because of tangled fibres. It would be better for beginners to avoid these and to choose a fleece with a staple length of 5½ in to 7 in. Look for the best and longest wool, remember to part the wool carefully, almost stroking the wool apart, and do not grab pieces of wool. For worsted threads, it is necessary to be very discriminating.

Matchings

It is sometimes possible to buy a fleece which has already been graded; it is known as 'matchings'. If, for example, all 56s quality was required, it could be bought from a specialist supplier.

Another method of sorting

Jane Goodyear, an experienced spinner and teacher of spinning, uses a method of sorting which takes into account the fact that a sheep usually sleeps on the same side. This

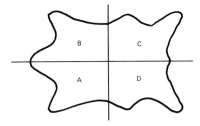

Figure 2.3. Another method of wool-sorting

means that one half of the fleece will be more exposed to the weather. When sorting, she divides the fleece into four parts – A, B, C, and D. The dirty edges are sorted off, and then the four sections are placed in separate boxes. In order to distribute the qualities, single threads are spun from each quarter and kept separate; then, when they are plied, A is plied with C, and B with D (*Figure 2.4*).

Storing wool

Store wool in an old cotton pillowcase. Tissue paper or newspaper can be used to separate the grades after sorting. Try not to buy more fleece than can be coped with in a year, because it might harden. However, fleece can sometimes be kept for several years and not deteriorate.

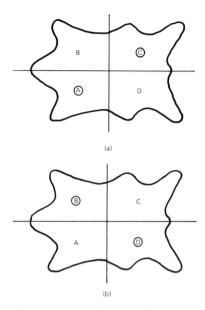

(a)

(b)

Figure 2.4. (a) Singles spun from sections C & A are plied. (b) Singles spun from sections B & D are plied

If a fleece has been scoured before storing, dry it thoroughly, wrap it in paper, and make sure it is labelled with the name of the breed and grade. Plastic bags are not generally recommended for storing fleece because wool retains moisture.

It is advisable to take precautions to prevent moths, for which a number of sprays are available. One spinner freezes her fleece to avoid trouble from moth damage.

3

Simple spinning

Woollen and worsted spinning

There are two basic types of thread: woollen and worsted. They result from the choice of fibre length, preparation (carding or combing), and the method of spinning. Between the woollen and worsted threads, there are those which are sometimes called 'semi-woollen' and 'semi-worsted'. The technique chosen should be one which is suitable for the fibre and for the end product.

Woollen threads should be soft, light, and airy. Air should be trapped in the fibres, making the resulting yarn resilient. Cloth from this kind of yarn will be particularly soft and warm.

Worsted threads are the result of careful choice of fibre and of combing. The fibres are kept as parallel as possible, and a sleek thread is the result.

Spinning is the process of converting a raw material into a thread or yarn. The words 'thread' and 'yarn' are interchangeable, as are the words 'twist' and 'spin'.

Finger spinning

Finger spinning is one of the best ways of getting to know fleece. It enables a spinner to understand the qualities of a particular wool, and it gives a designer the opportunity to

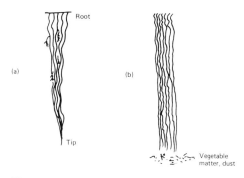

Figure 3.1. (a) A lock of wool. (b) Separated or teased fibres

Figure 3.2. One method of finger twisting

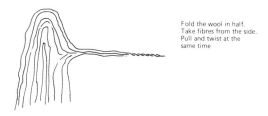

Figure 3.3. Another method of finger twisting

experiment in hundreds of ways. As the term suggests, we use our fingers to spin a yarn. The method is as follows.

Take a lock of wool. Separate the fibres so that any vegetable matter or burrs fall out (*Figure 3.1*). Pull out a few fibres and at the same time twist them, almost as if winding up a watch (*Figure 3.2*). As you pull, twist. Fibres will cling to each other, and a long thread will result, until it is impossible to stretch the arm any farther.

Another method of finger spinning is shown in *Figure 3.3*.

27

These two methods will allow thick threads, thin threads, tightly twisted, loosely twisted, lustrous, non-lustrous, and coloured threads to be spun (*Figures 3.4* and *3.5*).

The single thread which is produced is known as 'singles'.

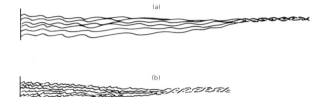

Figure 3.4. (a) Smooth, lustrous thread, twisted from Lincoln fleece. (b) Soft, spongy and springy yarn twisted from Southdown fleece

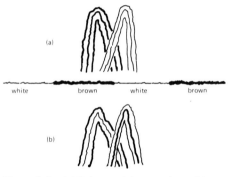

white   brown   white   brown

Figure 3.5. (a) Colour mixing so that white and brown fibres are used separately, giving a yarn with white and brown lengths. (b) Brown and white are mixed, giving a blend of colour

Plied yarn
When a single thread is doubled (folded back on itself), it becomes two-ply. Give the singles thread plenty of twist and then let it fold back on itself (*Figure 3.6*).

Designing finger-spun yarns
The raw material itself forms a perfect source of inspiration. Wool provides numerous opportunities for the designer, but

28

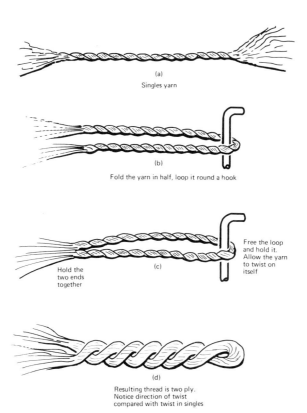

(a)

Singles yarn

(b)

Fold the yarn in half, loop it round a hook

(c)

Hold the
two ends
together

Free the loop
and hold it.
Allow the yarn
to twist on
itself

(d)

Resulting thread is two ply.
Notice direction of twist
compared with twist in singles

Figure 3.6. Doubling yarn

one must not forget the possibilities suggested by other raw materials, used on their own or blended. The softness of silk, the unyielding stiffness and strength of flax, or the challenge of synthetic fibres in staple form, all offer suggestions to the designer.

When mixing fibres, it is necessary to consider the ultimate use of the blend and whether it is going to be washed. For decorative hangings where washing does not have to be considered there are endless ways of mixing, blending, twisting, plaiting, knotting, and binding.

29

When looking for new ideas, consider the form and shape of grasses and weeds in the fields. Look at the structure of the stems, buds, or seeds, and at their silhouettes against the sky.

Subtle colour changes are very suitable for natural coloured fleece, while bright clear colours suggest ways of using oddments left over from dyeing experiments.

Once the joy of finger-spinning has been discovered, endless possibilities occur. There is no need for a spindle, carders, or a spinning-wheel – all that is needed is some raw material, fingers, and a seeing eye.

Figure 3.7. Garment knitted in New Zealand from finger-twisted yarn

Children can make all kinds of textured threads, which can be used in embroidery, knitting, or weaving. They need a little encouragement, but young children particularly are very inventive and will soon experience the pleasure of feeling the threads form in their fingers as they twist and manipulate the fibres.

Knitting with finger-spun wool
Many New Zealand knitters make beautiful hats, sweaters, and scarves by finger-twisting wool (*Figure 3.7*). Threads can be twisted to the desired thickness: experienced knitters judge the equivalent thicknesses of yarns and choose appropriate knitting patterns, but beginners should practise finger-spinning and make something simple, such as a bag or scarf, which does not have to be an exact size. Squares could be knitted and joined together.

The method is shown in *Figure 3.8*. Twist a length of fleece and start to cast on stitches, using size 8 needles. As the length is used up, twist on another piece. Start by trying to twist a length of about 6 in, cast on the stitches, and continue knitting. Every time the thread has been used up, twist another length on. Remember to allow sufficient overlap for the join.

The method is very simple, once the technique has been understood. The textures, colours, and yarns can be used either in a predetermined pattern or in a random way.

Finger-spun yarn for weaving
Threads of different lengths, colours, and textures can be spun with the fingers and used when making tapestries. They can also be added as decorative knots.

Spindle spinning

The next stage in learning to spin is to make a continuous thread, which is easier with a spindle. A spindle consists of a stick with a weight at the bottom, known as the 'whorl'.

31

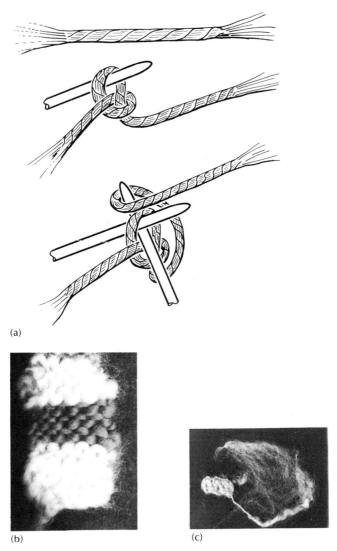

(a)

(b)   (c)

Figure 3.8. (a) Knitting with finger-twisted yarn. (b) Knitting with finger-twisted combed wool. (c) Crochet with finger-spun wool

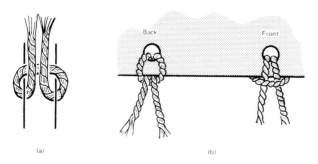

Figure 3.9. (a) Knots added to a warp. (b) Fringe

A spindle has many advantages: it can be used for all fibres; threads can vary from the finest to the thickest; it is easy to make; very little storage space is required; and it can be carried around with one and is always ready to be used.

Choice of the weight of a spindle is influenced by the length and strength of the fibre to be spun and the thickness of the required thread. A fine, lightly twisted thread will require a light spindle, while a thick thread will need a heavier weight. When very fine fibres, such as cotton, are being spun, it is advisable to rest the tip of the spindle in a bowl so that the weight of the whorl will not break the thread.

It is possible to make a simple spindle by pushing a knitting needle through a wooden cotton reel, or a stick through a lump of clay, an apple, or a potato. Whorls can vary in weight, but one weighing about 1 oz would be suitable for a beginner. Most suppliers of spinning and weaving equipment sell spindles.

Preparing a spindle

A length of yarn, called the 'leader' or 'starter yarn', has to be attached to the stem of the spindle. The yarn can be finger-twisted and tied to the stem, but it will be easier to begin with a hairy machine-made thread at first. It should be twisted in

33

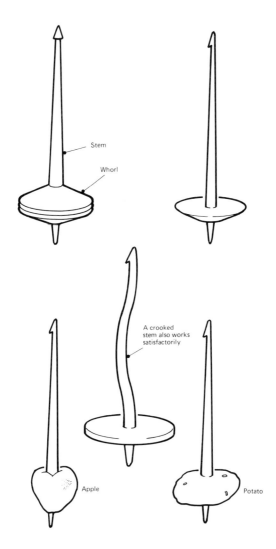

Stem

Whorl

A crooked
stem also works
satisfactorily

Apple

Potato

Figure 3.10. Spindles

34

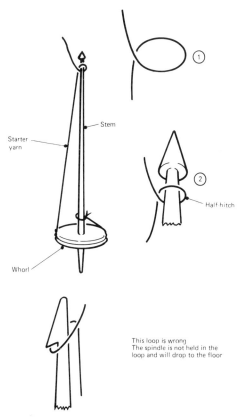

Starter
yarn

Stem

Whorl

Half-hitch

This loop is wrong
The spindle is not held in the
loop and will drop to the floor

Figure 3.11. Preparing a spindle

the same direction as the thread which is to be spun; if it is
not, the thread will disintegrate, have no strength, and break.

Woollen fibres may be uncarded, carded, or combed (see
Chapter 4), according to the type of thread required.

Spinning from the fleece
Take a handful of unwashed fleece, preferably of a medium-
length staple. Pull the fibres apart gently in order to loosen
them and to allow vegetable matter, dead insects, or seeds to

fall out. The method of joining the fleece to the leader is shown in *Figure 3.13*. The important thing is to allow plenty of overlap: the fibres are very ready to cling together if given the chance.

With the fibres overlapping the leader, hold them firmly between the left finger and thumb. Give the top of the spindle a quick turn to the right (clockwise) with the right hand. This movement will make the twist come up the leader thread, joining the fleece and leader (*Figure 3.14*). Watch the twist come up and see how the woollen fibres cling to the leader.

The distance travelled by the twist has to be controlled: it must not be allowed to run into the fibres before they have been drawn out (drafted). The left finger and thumb can be in control: by closing them together, the twist can be halted at that point.

At first, the twist either will not go far enough or will go too far. Once the right balance is obtained between the amount of twist and the distance it is allowed to travel, all will be well.

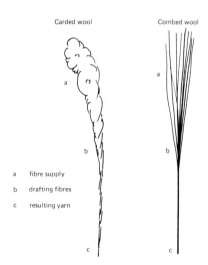

Carded wool   Combed wool

a   fibre supply

b   drafting fibres

c   resulting yarn

Figure 3.12. The three essential processes in spinning

36

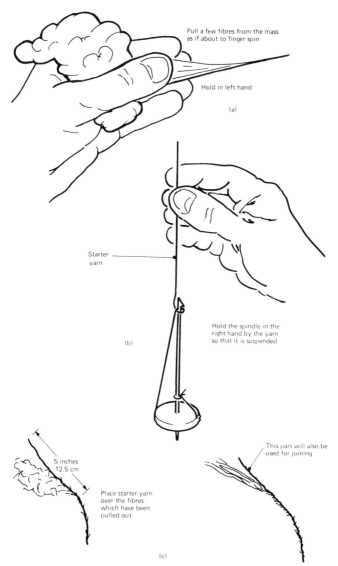

Pull a few fibres from the mass as if about to finger spin

Hold in left hand

(a)

Starter yarn

Hold the spindle in the right hand by the yarn so that it is suspended

(b)

5 inches 12.5 cm

Place starter yarn over the fibres which have been pulled out

This part will also be used for joining

(c)

Figure 3.13. Joining the fleece

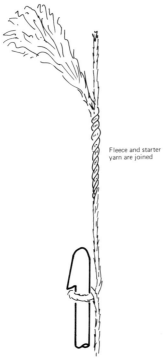

Fleece and starter
yarn are joined

Figure 3.14. Close-up of the join

Do not be concerned about the type of thread produced at first. Concentrate on keeping the spindle turning in a clockwise direction, and pulling out sufficient fleece to form a strong thread.

Continue as follows.

Turn the spindle to the right with the right hand while the left hand is stopping the spin from travelling into the fleece.

Move the right hand up to take over just below the left hand.

The left hand takes hold of the fibres about 2 in away from the right hand. (The distance between the hands will differ according to the length of the staple. Long-stapled wool will need the hands to be farther apart; with a short-stapled wool, the hands will have to stay closer.)

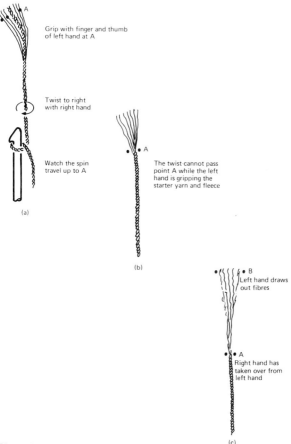

Grip with finger and thumb
of left hand at A

Twist to right
with right hand

Watch the spin
travel up to A

(a)

The twist cannot pass
point A while the left
hand is gripping the
starter yarn and fleece

(b)

Left hand draws
out fibres

Right hand has
taken over from
left hand

(c)

Figure 3.15. Starting to spin

Draw fibres down with the right hand. At this stage, the thickness of the thread is being decided.

Allow the twist to travel upwards by opening the right finger and thumb.

Be ready to stop the twist with the left finger and thumb.

After a little practice, it should be possible to turn the spindle with the right hand and then draw the fibres down with the same hand several times before having to turn the spindle. Make sure the spindle does not turn backwards.

The spindle will want to spin backwards, so try to give a good twist each time and remember to watch the whorl for signs of untwisting.

Underspinning – insufficient twist in the yarn – can be caused by drawing out too long a draft and not allowing enough twist to travel up. There will be no strength, and the wool will break.

Overspinning has the opposite cause: the draft was short and there was too much twist for the length. The thread will curl and twist on itself. In weaving, this could have disastrous effects on the width of the cloth because, after washing, the tightly twisted weft would pull the material in. (However, this effect might be wanted in decorative work.)

Another difficulty is twist travelling into the fleece. This will happen if one hand is lazy and does not stop the twist in time. It can be extremely difficult to pull out the fibres when they have been twisted, but it will be much easier if they are turned the other way. If the fleece has become twisted, stop the spindle, untwist the thick thread, and pull the fibres in order to spread the spin over a longer length.

At first, it is important to try to control the movement and direction of the spindle and the amount of twist, and to achieve the right difference between the firm grip of the fingers and thumbs and the relaxed movement of the hand holding the fleece.

Whenever the thread breaks or disintegrates, take the end of the spun thread and spread out the fibres before trying to join them into the fleece. Try to anticipate a broken thread, and do not hope that the thin part of the yarn will not break. (It may not break until a skein is being made, and then it will be a nuisance.) When joining, make sure there is plenty of overlap, otherwise the weight of the spindle will drag the fibres apart.

When a long length of thread has been spun and the arms cannot stretch any farther, the thread must be wound on to the stem of the spindle. This is done as follows.

Loosely wind the spun thread round the left hand until it is within about 5 in of the top of the spindle. Keep the thread taut. Slip the wool from the top of the spindle and from under the whorl.

Starting from the end of the stem nearest the whorl, wind the spun thread evenly round the spindle in a crosswise direction so that a cone-shape will eventually be formed. (By winding on rhythmically and evenly, the spun thread can easily be removed for winding, skeining, or plying. It also helps to keep a good balance on the spindle.) Leave a long enough length to allow for a half hitch to be made at the top of the stem with about 5 in to spare.

Spinning can continue until the spindle is comfortably full.

Direction of twist
So far, the spindle has been turned to the right. If the thread is allowed to hang vertically, it will be seen to have a twist running from top right to bottom left, as in a letter Z. It is easy to remember that a Z twist results when the spindle is turned to the right, because one writes a letter Z from left to right.

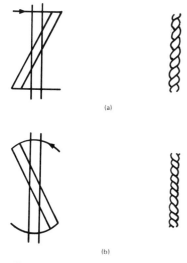

(a)

(b)

Figure 3.16. (a) Z twist. (b) S twist

41

If the spindle is turned from right to left, the opposite twist results. This is called the S twist, a letter S being written from right to left.

Never try to spin an S twist and a Z twist on the same length of thread because obviously the first length will untwist and disintegrate.

Taking the wool from the spindle

There are several ways of taking the wool from the spindle. If the wool is to be washed and dyed, a well-organised skein is required, but if it is going to be plied, it can be wound into a ball or on to a bobbin.

Push up the whorl carefully so that the spun wool is removed in a compact cone. Slip this cone over a knitting needle in place of the stem of the spindle. A home-made stand to receive the cones can be made by pushing knitting needles through a piece of plywood or firm polystyrene. The wool can then be used from the cone without getting it into a tangle.

When making a skein, it is worth taking trouble. If it is useful to know the yardage obtained from a given weight of wool, decide on a definite length of skein (e.g., ½ yd or ½ m), so that once round the skein is one unit of length.

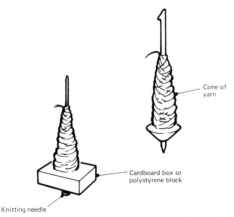

Figure 3.17. The cone of yarn is placed on a knitting needle

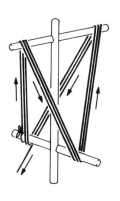 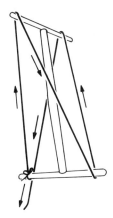

Figure 3.18. A niddy-noddy

A piece of equipment called a 'niddy-noddy' is used for skeining. It consists of two pieces of wood fixed to a third (*Figure 3.18*). By winding in the direction indicated by the arrows, it is possible to obtain a well-made measured skein.

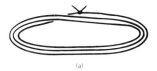 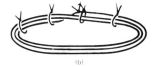

(a)   (b)

Figure 3.19. Tying skeins

While the completed skein is still in position, tie the beginning and end together. Do not take them round the skein. Attach a separate thread to one of the ends and tie it round the skein loosely. This separate thread should be of a different type so that it is easily distinguishable from the rest. Tie two more threads in two evenly spaced places.

These ties will help to keep the thread in order when it goes through the processes of washing, rinsing, dyeing, and drying. They must be securely tied but not too loose or too tight.

Figure 3.20.   Skein tied too tightly

Figure 3.21.   Skein tied correctly

Figure 3.22.   Skein tied too loosely

Figure 3.23.   A safer way of tying skeins

Another method of tying is shown in *Figure 3.23*.

After washing the skeins, they should be dried under tension.

4

Carding, combing, scouring and spindle spinning

Carding

For this process, two carders are needed. A carder consists of a piece of wood covered with little bent wires fastened to leather, and a handle (*Figure 4.1*). Choose carders which have a smooth, curved back, because that enables one to roll the wool on the back.

Label one carder A and one B (or one left and right). It is customary always to use them in the same hands.

Take a fleece, and tease the wool by holding a small amount in the left hand and separating the fibres with the

Figure 4.1. A pair of carders

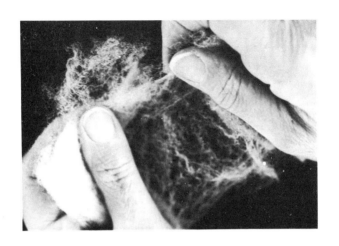

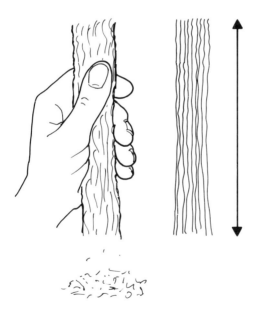

Figure 4.2. Teasing

right hand (*Figure 4.2*) until the fibres are more or less parallel.

Sit down, and place the teased wool on carder A from the handle downwards. If it is long, let it hang over the edge of the carder, not over the handle end. Cover the wires lightly with wool so that there is a filmy layer over them, starting with a small handful. If there is too much wool on the carder, it becomes difficult to handle, but if there is not enough, the fibres become wispy and almost get lost amongst the wires. There is a tendency to put too much wool on the carders.

Hold carder A in the left hand with the wooden back on the left knee and the palm of the hand facing upwards.

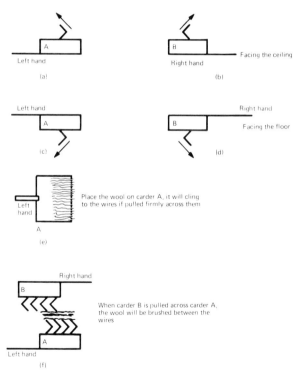

Figure 4.3. Carders, showing which way wires are bent

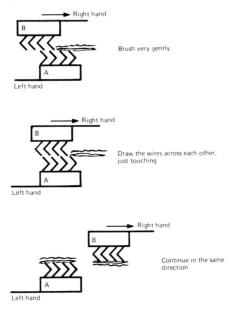

Figure 4.4. Starting to card wool

Take carder B in the right hand and hold it over carder A. Brush the wool gently, with the wires just touching as the carders are pulled across each other. Repeat this brushing at least three times. Use a big circular movement, so that there is no danger that the fibres will fold back on themselves.

The wool now has to be transferred from carder A to carder B. Turn carder B over (the wires are now upwards). Still

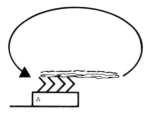

Figure 4.5. Making a circular movement with the carders

48

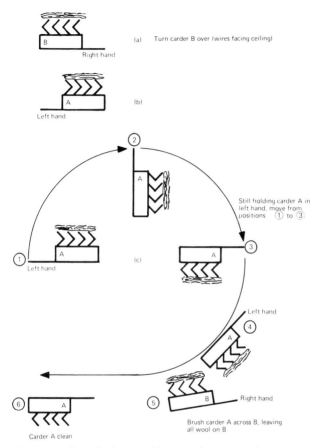

Figure 4.6. Transferring wool from carder A to carder B

holding carder A with the left hand, turn it over until the handle is pointing to the right and the wires are facing downwards. Place the edge of carder A against the handle end of carder B and brush away from the handle of carder B. The wool has now been transferred to carder B, and there should be none on A.

Brushing must be repeated. Place the clean carder A on the knee and brush carder B, which has all the wool on it, across A at least three times.

There are fibres on each carder now, and those on B must be transferred to A.

Hold the fringe of carder B against the edge of carder A (near the handle). Draw carder A across carder B, thus

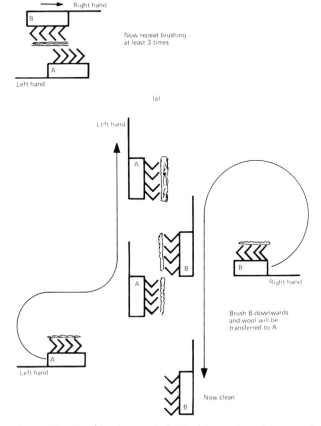

Figure 4.7. Brushing is repeated. Wool is transferred from carder B to carder A

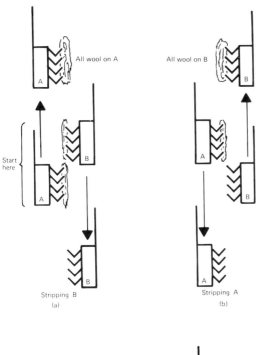

All wool on A

All wool on B

Start here

Stripping B
(a)

Stripping A
(b)

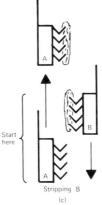

Start here

Stripping B
(c)

Figure 4.8. Stripping the carders

51

transferring all the wool to A. Repeat the brushing several times, until the wool is evenly carded, with no lumps in it.

If the fibres have been successfully transferred from A to B and B to A during carding, it should not be difficult to remove them complete (*Figure 4.8*). If the veil of wool can be passed from one carder to the other without a tangle resulting (*Figure 4.9*) it should be lifted gently on to the back of the carder, as it is ready for rolling.

Figure 4.9. Passing the fleece from one carder to the other

Making a rolag
The roll of wool which is about to be made is called a 'rolag' (*Figure 4.10*).

The layer of wool on the back of the carder should just fit; do not make it spread out.

Place the hand on the wool, using the little finger down to the wrist, to hold the wool in position while the wooden top of the other carder is used to roll the wool up. Roll the wool up gradually so that there is a little tube of air in the middle. The last wispy fibres should curl round until it is impossible to tell where the rolag begins and ends. Once a rolag has been made, treat it gently.

In carding, the most important thing is to understand the angle of the wires and what happens when the carders are brushed away from each other and towards each other. Also check when the wires are facing upwards or downwards.

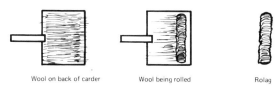

Wool on back of carder   Wool being rolled   Rolag

Figure 4.10.   Making rolags

Combing

Start with a lustrous wool with a staple length of 6 in to 8 in and try a simple way of combing.
Choose a lock and tease the fibres with the fingers. Keep the fibres parallel (*Figure 4.11*).

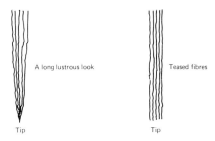

A long lustrous look   Teased fibres

Tip   Tip

Figure 4.11.   Teasing the wool, keeping the fibres parallel

A dog comb can be clamped to a table so that the wool can be taken, one staple at a time, through the teeth of the comb. Short fibres (called 'noils') will be left in the comb. Remove these and use them to mix with other fibres. Place the combed staples together; the tips can be kept together, or the direction of the fibres can be mixed.

53

Scouring

Fleece is very smelly, dirty, and greasy, so when should it be scoured (washed)? There are two schools of thought on this.

The fleece can be left just as it is, and it is spun direct from the locks or it is carded. Grease, dirt, and smell are all retained and have to be removed later. Alternatively, the grease, dirt and smell are removed by scouring before the fleece is spun. Oil is usually added before spinning.

The arguments for spinning 'in the grease' are as follows. The yarns are more elastic; it is more thrifty. Fleece is easier to spin when retaining its natural oil, as the lanolin helps the fibres to slide past each other, so that a constant amount is spun – this is particularly true of freshly shorn fleece.

On the other hand, the dirt, having been washed away, will not be trapped in the fibres as they are spun. The yarn will not need a great deal of washing before dyeing. Fleece can be dyed before spinning for blended colours. And washed fleece is more pleasant to handle.

Wool must be absolutely clean and free from grease before being dyed if a level colour is required. (If an unevenly dyed yarn is required, add some grease to the wool.)

Scouring wool
Start by steeping the wool. Prepare clean water at 120°F–130°F (50°C–55°C). It will feel hot to the hands. Place the skeins or fleece in the water. Fleece should be tied in thin muslin or plastic netting. While it is in the bath, untie the muslin or netting and gently move the fleece about. Skeins should be hung through a tape, then the tape tied to the handles of the bath. Allow the wool to steep until the water is cold. Avoid agitating the wool.

Make a good lather in hot water with soap or detergent.

When the water is cool enough to put the hand into it comfortably, immerse the wool. Move it gently around in the water; it should not be compressed. Avoid rubbing or washing the wool as this could encourage it to felt.

The wool can be left in the suds overnight, then gently rinsed in lukewarm water with vinegar added if soap has been used.

The number of times the wool has to be treated like this depends on its degree of greasiness at the beginning. If it is very dirty and greasy, it may be necessary to repeat the scouring three or four times. Use less soap each time.

Make sure the wool is well rinsed. It can be partly dried in a spin drier, inside an old pillowcase. Do not use a tumbler drier. If the wool is to be dyed straight away, keep it damp, because this will avoid the need to wet it out.

If a very pale, delicate colour is required, it may be necessary to bleach the wool. A weak solution of hydrogen peroxide should be used.

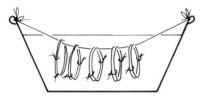

Figure 4.12. Skeins tied on tape

Scouring other animal hair
These materials are unlikely to be as greasy as sheep's wool, so a light wash in soapy water will probably be sufficient.

Oiling

If spinning wool 'in the grease', it may not be necessary to add any oil at all because there may be plenty of lanolin on the wool already. This will depend on the type of fleece, when it was shorn, how long the fleece has been stored, and how and where it was stored. But some natural wool can feel dry and dusty, and wool from the end of the fleece towards the tail can feel rather dry, especially if it comes from a sheep that has been out in wet and windy weather on a mountainside.

A beginner might find it easier to add a little oil anyway, because it will help the fibres to cling together while being spun. But beware of putting too much oil on. A little olive oil on the fingertips is usually sufficient. After teasing the wool, just place the fleece on the carders with slightly oiled fingertips; three drops of olive oil will go a long way.

Another way is to tease a pile of wool and then spray it with a little oil, using a scentspray or garden spray. Then pull the fibres apart gently to allow the oil to spread. The wool can be oiled like this, wrapped in newspaper, and carded next day.

Corn oil or other vegetable oils have a tendency to become sticky and may stain the fibres. They may also make the wool smell unpleasant and the smell of some will not wash out.

It is usually necessary to add oil to scoured or dyed wool, but some spinners seem to be able to spin very satisfactorily without doing so.

Oil can be applied in the form of an emulsion. Dissolve 4oz washing soda in ½gall of water and add this to neatsfoot oil until a milky emulsion is formed. A saucer of this mixture can be kept near the wheel and the fingers dipped into it while spinning. Or the mixture can be put into a spray and sprinkled evenly over the fleece. If the fleece is sprayed and then left for a day or two before carding or spinning, the oil will become evenly distributed. After spinning, give the wool a good wash to remove all traces of the oil.

Neatsfoot oil can be bought from saddlers.

Using a spindle with a rolag
It is likely to be much easier to get an even thread when using a rolag. To make a woollen thread with a long draw, prepare the spindle with a starter yarn, which should be fairly rough and strong; singles thread should be Z-twisted. The rolag is light and airy, so if it is stretched and a little twist added to give it strength, it should make a soft and airy thread. The amount of twist will determine the kind of yarn, and the

purpose for which the yarn is required will decide the kind to be made.

It is easier to make a hard-twisted yarn than a light and airy one. Judging the length of draft, the amount of twist, and the right moment to let the twist run up the fibres takes practice. If one is tense and anxious about the spindle dropping or turning backwards, the yarn will be hard, uneven and tightly twisted. The finger and thumb of the left hand should hold a few fibres from the rolag and the starter thread together. The rolag should lie over the back of the hand in an undisturbed way. Give the top of the spindle a quick turn to the right. Keep hold of the rolag and the starter yarn until the spin has

Rolag

Figure 4.13. Joining the rolag to the leader yarn

travelled up and joined them securely. Allow plenty of overlap, better too much than too little.

Keep the rolag over the left hand. Before twisting the spindle to the right again with the right hand, nip the rolag at the point where the twist stops, using the left hand. In *Figure*

4.14 the arrow shows how far the twist has travelled. This twist will continue upwards when the spindle is turned again, unless the finger and thumb of the left hand stop it. While holding the juncture of yarn and rolag with the left hand, turn

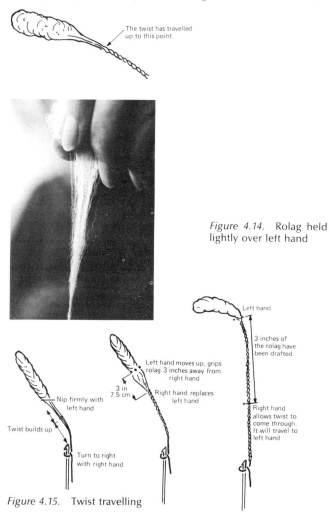

The twist has travelled up to this point

Figure 4.14. Rolag held lightly over left hand

Left hand

3 inches of the rolag have been drafted

Left hand moves up, grips rolag 3 inches away from right hand

3 in
7.5 cm

Right hand replaces left hand

Right hand allows twist to come through. It will travel to left hand

Nip firmly with left hand

Twist builds up

Turn to right with right hand

Figure 4.15. Twist travelling

the spindle to the right and immediately the right hand should take over just below the left hand. Twist will be building up between the top of the spindle and the right hand. The left hand, having given up its position to the right hand, grips the rolag about 3 in away from the right hand and starts to draft the fibres. As these fibres are drawn upwards, the twist will travel up, but there will not be enough twist unless the right hand allows more twist to come through the finger and thumb (*Figure 4.15*).

Keep practising this method of woollen spinning until the amount of twisting and drafting can be controlled and a soft lightly twisted yarn is produced. A very sensitive touch is required so that the twist goes where and when it is wanted. If the thread breaks, tease out the end and overlap the fibres (*Figure 4.16*).

Tease out the end before joining

These ends cannot be joined

Figure 4.16. Joining

When joining a new rolag, always leave off before getting right to the end of the old one; then the new rolag can blend into the old without an obvious join.

To spin a thick, loosely twisted thread, make a small rolag and join it to the starter yarn. Hold the rolag in the left hand and build up a large amount of twist between the top of the spindle and the beginning of the rolag (*Figure 4.17*). Hold the top of the spindle with the right hand and keep the twist back while the left hand takes the end of the rolag and drafts it into a thick thread. A small amount of twist must be allowed through the right finger and thumb to stop the wool disintegrating.

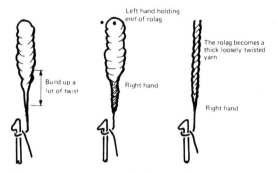

Figure 4.17. Spinning a thick thread

Spinning a semi-woollen thread is easier. Join as before, but use a short draw. Instead of drafting by pulling the left hand upwards, the right hand pulls the fibres downwards (*Figure 4.18*). This type of thread is suitable for warps, as it is strong and hard.

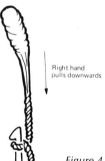

Figure 4.18. Spinning a semi-woollen thread

In the long draw, the left hand was drafting the fibres. Try reversing the actions so that the left hand turns the spindle in an anti-clockwise direction and the right hand drafts the fibres. A thread with an S-twist will be spun. (It is the right hand which usually does the drafting when using a spinning-wheel.)

Worsted spinning on a spindle
Prepare the spindle in the usual way by tying on a starter
yarn. Hold the combed wool in the left hand (*Figure 4.19*).

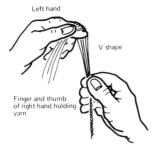

Left hand

V shape

Finger and thumb
of right hand holding
yarn

Figure 4.19.   Holding combed wool

Turn the spindle clockwise (for Z twist). The right hand and
left hand work at the same time. Immediately after twisting
the spindle, take the right hand up to the point where the
twist stops. In *Figure 4.20* the V-shape is being extended by
the right hand carefully drawing away from the left hand. The
hands are gradually getting farther apart so that the right
thickness is being drafted. The spindle bears the weight of

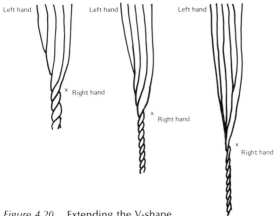

Left hand

x Right hand

Left hand

x
Right hand

Left hand

x
Right hand

Figure 4.20.   Extending the V-shape

61

the fibres. The right hand moves up the fibres, smoothing them and feeling the twist going up (*Figure 4.21*).

The rhythm is as follows. *1* Draw with left finger and thumb nearly closed; *2* right finger and thumb closed (no spin can pass); *3* run the right finger and thumb upwards, nearly closed – the left finger and thumb are closed.

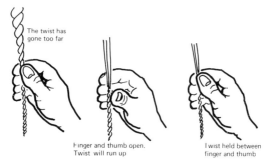

Figure 4.21. The twist moves up

Remember to keep the spindle revolving, to hold the fibres in the left hand in a fan or V-shape, and to keep an even tension. Both hands move away from each other when drafting, which must be done carefully to maintain an even thread: a tug on the fibres will cause a break, insufficient pull will make a thick thread, and too much pull will result in a very fine thread. The length of staple will determine the length of draw; 2 in will probably be the maximum (*Figure 4.22*).

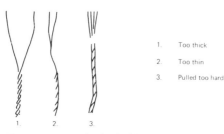

1. Too thick
2. Too thin
3. Pulled too hard

Figure 4.22. Faults in drafting

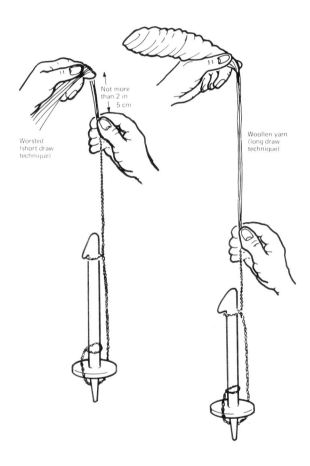

Worsted
(short draw
technique)

Not more
than 2 in
5 cm

Woollen yarn
(long draw
technique)

Figure 4.23. Difference in actions when spinning woollen and worsted

63

Spinning with uncarded wool

Wool can be spun without carding or combing. Locks of wool are taken from a sorted fleece; they are held in the left hand and gently pulled apart so that they form a kind of roving which measures 1 yd (*Figure 4.24*).

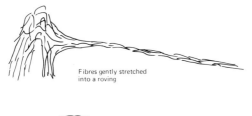

Fibres gently stretched
into a roving

60 of these rovings are placed in a basket

Figure 4.24.   Making rovings

The roving is lightly wound up, and placed in a basket. When spun, 60 such rovings will fill a bobbin and weigh about 3 oz (when washed, about 2 oz).

As the fibres were not taken parallel to each other, a woollen thread will be spun from the rovings.

5

Spinning-wheels

The development of the spinning-wheel from the spindle is shown in *Figure 5.1*. There are many theories concerning the first wheels and where they were made, but it is probable that the spindle wheel (*Figure 5.3*) was invented in India between AD 500 and AD 1000. There has been a revival of interest in the spindle wheel (otherwise known as the long, muckle, Welsh, or great wheel), but if buying one remember that it needs a fairly large space when being used (*Figure 5.4*). The other basic type is the Saxony wheel, which was invented by Johann Jurgen, a German, in 1530. It is also known as the flyer, long-fibre, or flax wheel. Its great advantage over the great wheel is that drafting, twisting, and winding on take place at the same time.

Spinning on the great wheel
The great wheel, when used correctly, will enable a spinner to produce a wide variety of threads, ranging from a very fine worsted to rough-textured, thick yarns.

Tie a length of Z-twisted spun yarn to the spindle about half-way down its length and hold it at an angle of 45 degrees to the spindle. Rotating the spindle will make the yarn spiral up it, and when it reaches the point, the yarn will slip off. Each time it slips off, one turn of twist has been inserted in the length of yarn.

Short or very short fibres can be spun on this wheel, using the following method.

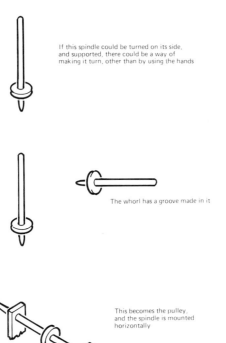

If this spindle could be turned on its side, and supported, there could be a way of making it turn, other than by using the hands

The whorl has a groove made in it

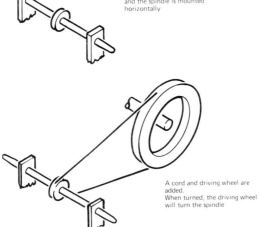

This becomes the pulley, and the spindle is mounted horizontally

A cord and driving wheel are added.
When turned, the driving wheel will turn the spindle

Figure 5.1. Development of the spindle wheel

Figure 5.2. Drop spindle and spinning-wheel being used in Park High School, Pontefract (photo, H. Huby)

Figure 5.3. The 'great wheel' (photo, Bankfield Museum, Halifax)

Figure 5.4. Spinning on the 'great wheel' (photo, Bankfield Museum, Halifax)

Rotate the wheel slowly. Draw the hand away for a distance of 3 ft to 5 ft. Rotate the wheel to give the required amount of twist. The wheel is backed off and the hand is moved until the yarn is at right-angles to the spindle. To 'back off' means to reverse the spindle direction to unwind the yarn that has spiralled up to the spindle point. The yarn is wound on, and the hand returns to the drafting position, leaving about 18in of yarn between the spindle and the hand.

Modern spinning-wheels

There are many types of spinning-wheels in use today, and with the increasing popularity of hand-spinning, a large number of manufacturers are developing new designs. Wheels can mostly be divided into two groups: those with a double driving-band, such as the Saxony wheel, many of which are manufactured in Scandinavia; and those with a single driving-band and a bobbin brake, among which the Ashford wheel is very popular.

The Saxony wheel
A large number of wheels are based on the Saxony design (*Figure 5.5*) which consists of the following parts.

The *table* is made from a strong block of wood; it is approximately rectangular in shape.

The *driving wheel* is the most distinctive feature. At the centre is the *hub*, a round block of wood through which the axle passes. The *rim* of the wheel has raised outer edges to stop the driving-band from slipping off. Two uprights fixed to the right of the table support the *axle*, which is kept in place by wooden pegs. Always make sure they are firmly fixed. Wooden caps are unscrewed to oil the axle or remove the wheel. On the back of the axle there is a crank which is fixed to the treadle by the *footman* (*pitman*). This is usually a wooden rod, attached to (but not touching) the *treadle* by a leather thong or a strong piece of cord. Sometimes a piece of cord is used instead of a wooden rod.

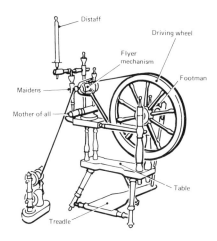

Figure 5.5. Swedish spinning wheel (drawing, Bankfield Museum, Halifax)

The *mother-of-all* consists of a round disc with a crossbar. This bar holds the two uprights known as *maidens*, which in turn hold the leather bearings for the *flyer* mechanism. The back maiden is fixed, probably glued, in position, but the front maiden has to be free to move so that it can be twisted round to allow the flyer to be removed. (Having removed the flyer, always make sure the maiden is turned back into the correct position: i.e., the leather bearing should be at right-angles to the support.) On some wheels, the maiden can slide along the mother-of-all and is fixed by a wooden nut which must be loosened when necessary. Always make sure the maidens are parallel to each other. The *tensioner* enables the mother-of-all to be moved backwards and forwards, thus altering the tension of the driving-band.

The *flyer mechanism* consists of the following components.

The *spindle* is a solid metal shaft with an open end, through which the yarn passes, called the *orifice*. The diameter of the orifice can influence the size of the yarn, as a thick yarn will obviously not go through a small orifice. Near

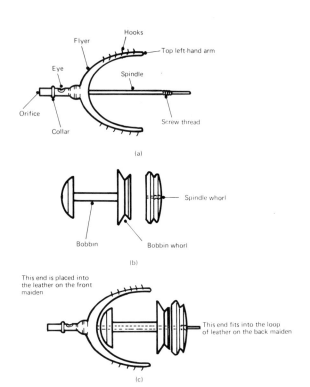

Figure 5.6. The flyer mechanism. (a, b) Components. (c) Flyer ready to be put in position

the end there is a screw-thread, usually a left-hand thread because the spindle is turned clockwise, on to which the *spindle whorl* is screwed. In the spindle whorl there may be two grooves, one deeper than the other, giving the spinner a choice of position for the driving-band. The shallower groove may be intended for use when plying and the deeper one for spinning, or the shallow one may be for weft threads and the deeper one for warp threads.

On the arms of the flyer there are *hooks* (*hecks*) which are used to guide the spun thread as it is wound on to the *bobbin*. The bobbin is separate from the spindle. It has a grooved whorl at one end, and, at the end which fits into the flyer, a dome-shaped disc. The stem of the bobbin is hollow and should fit comfortably on the spindle shaft – if too tight, it will not move, and if too loose, it will slip. If it slips and brings the driving-band close to the flyer arms, the cord could catch on the end hook. If this is likely to happen, place a washer on the spindle before putting on the bobbin. When putting the bobbin on the spindle shaft, place the whorl next to the spindle whorl and not at the other end.

Bobbins are removed from the spindle by slipping off the driving-band and unscrewing the spindle whorl. It is not always necessary to remove bobbins, as yarn can be wound into skeins, balls, or spools quite easily by slipping both ends of the driving-band on to the spindle whorl. This allows the bobbin to run freely, and the yarn can be wound without any trouble. When starting to spin again, remember to slip the driving-band back into position, or the wool will not wind on and a long, over-twisted yarn will result.

The *driving-band* forms the connection between the spinning unit (spindle, bobbin, and flyer) and the wheel. A double driving-band consists of a long, strong piece of string, thin very soft cord, or nylon. As a strong band which does not stretch is necessary, many spinners use nylon.

One long band

Band doubled in half showing crossing

Figure 5.7. The driving band

The cord is doubled in half, and the ends are stitched, spliced, or (preferably for the beginner) tied. The driving-band cannot be made to an exact size because it can be affected by humidity, unless it is nylon, and different tensions are needed according to the type of thread being spun. Incorrect tension of the driving-band can make spinning impossible; for example, a very tight band makes the thread disappear through the orifice too rapidly, whereas a slack band slows down the movement to almost nothing and an over-twisted, hard yarn will result. If fibres which are short and slippery are being used, a slack driving-band may be required.

The driving-band goes round the driving-wheel twice – once round the spindle whorl and once round the bobbin whorl – so on the wheel it appears to be two separate bands.

When spinning, the spinner has to control the draw-in and the amount of twist. The diameter of the bobbin stem will increase as more wool is wound on to it. In order to compensate for this, increase the tension slightly so that more twist will be put into the yarn. If this is not done, the last part of the spinning will be softer than the beginning.

The ratio of twist to draw-in should be constant, and the spinner should be in control of the speed at which the thread is wound on the bobbin. It can be held back or allowed to wind on at will – if the wheel is satisfactorily adjusted.

Ratios Most spinning-wheel suppliers specify the ratio of the whorl to the driving-wheel. Otherwise, there are two ways of finding the ratio. Divide the circumference of the wheel by the circumference of the flyer whorl (a piece of string can be used for measuring); or divide the diameter of the wheel by the diameter of the spindle-whorl.

The ratio determines how many times the spindle will revolve for each revolution of the wheel; e.g., if the wheel has a 6:1 ratio for each revolution of the wheel, there will be six turns per inch when 1 in of fibre is twisted. Higher ratios mean it is possible to spin quickly.

Preparing to use the wheel Before starting to use the wheel, make sure it has been well oiled (see p. 77). Find a comfortable chair of a suitable height. If the wheel is on a polished floor, it may slip, so place a damp cloth under the legs or stick ridged plastic under each leg.

Check that the driving-band is in the right place (over the spindle whorl and bobbin whorl).

If it is necessary to touch the wheel, always turn it by the spokes, as the driving-band could be knocked off if the rim is touched.

Before starting, it is important to ensure that the crank at the end of the axle is to the right of centre (2 o'clock).

It is easier to treadle if the foot is pressed flat against the treadle, so start without a shoe to make it possible to feel the wood on the sole of the foot. Keep the foot perfectly flat on the treadle.

Turn the wheel in a clockwise direction by touching a spoke, and practise treadling. Pedal quickly at first, pushing down firmly each time. Once a good rhythm has been achieved, slow down and keep the wheel turning while using the hands for something else, such as teasing wool, while treadling slowly.

If it is difficult to treadle, slacken the driving-band a little by moving the mother-of-all nearer the driving-wheel; check the position of the maidens; and make sure the footman is tied securely to the treadle.

If the wheel goes backwards, stop. Position the axle crank and start again.

If the wheel has been used by other spinners, check the spindle shaft and bobbin to make sure it is running smoothly. Slip off the driving-band, unscrew the spindle whorl, and take the bobbin off completely. The metal spindle shaft may be greasy and little pieces of spun wool may have got twisted round it, especially if the wheel has been used by someone who treadled irregularly. The thread may have slipped off the bobbin and twisted itself round the spindle between the disc of the bobbin and the curve of the flyer. Clean the metal shaft and return the bobbin, having made sure that the hole in the bobbin is clear. When replacing the spindle whorl, remember that it is probably on a left-hand thread.

Once the foot can control the wheel, think about the hand movements. In order to spin satisfactorily, the foot and the hands have to work together (particularly the thumb and index finger). If spinning has been practised on the spindle, the hand movements will not be difficult, as the feel of the wool and the twist will be familiar. It may help to give confidence if two fine machine-spun threads are plied together first, before starting to use fleece.

The Ashford wheel

Ashford wheels are manufactured in New Zealand. The Ashford has become one of the most popular wheels in the world because of its reasonable price, simplicity, and availability.

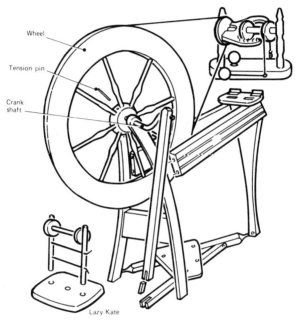

Figure 5.8. Ashford traditional wheel

The three main differences between a Saxony-type spinning-wheel and the Ashford wheel are that the Ashford has a single band and a brake ('Scotch tension'); there is no whorl at the end of the Ashford bobbin; and the mother-of-all is hinged and moves up and down.

On a wheel with a double driving-band, the whorl has to be unscrewed in order to take off the bobbin, but with the Ashford the bobbin can be removed by just turning the maiden and slipping off the brake.

Beginners often find the single-band wheel easy to use because the cord does not jump off with irregular treadling as often as a double driving-band does.

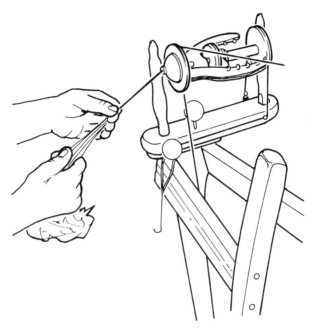

Figure 5.9. Spinning the first yarn on an Ashford wheel

Using the Ashford wheel   Most of the general hints already given apply.

Make sure the wheel has been well oiled and keep it oiled every three to four hours while working. Use a light oil or neatsfoot oil (which is suitable for leather and also for oiling wool). The parts to be oiled are: the axle bearing; the two bearings on the maidens (if leather); the bearings which carry the treadle; the leather connection between footman and treadle; and the spindle on which the bobbin rotates. Do not over-oil this, just rub it with an oily cloth so that the bobbin can run smoothly.

Once the driving-band is at the right tension, it will hardly ever need to be changed. This is because the brake can easily be altered in order to change the speed of winding-on.

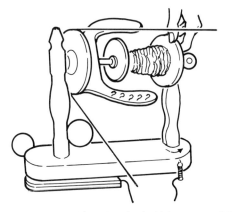

Figure 5.10. Changing the bobbin on an Ashford wheel

Make sure the supports holding the spindle shaft are at right-angles. If they are not correctly aligned, there will either be rubbing or the flyer may fall to the floor.

Practise treadling before starting to spin in order to develop a good rhythm.

Buying a wheel

Wheels can be quite expensive, so it is advisable to make sure that you are going to enjoy spinning on a particular wheel. It is possible to try out spinning-wheels by going to classes or to Weavers' Guild meetings. Beginners must gain as much experience as possible and talk to as many spinners as they can. When the Association of Guilds of Weavers holds summer schools in the UK, they arrange trade stalls, and at least a whole day is set aside for traders to bring their goods and equipment. On such days one can try out various

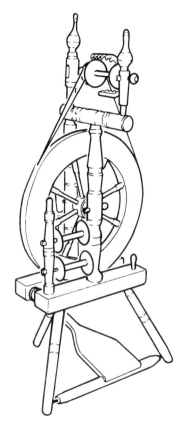

Figure 5.11. Shetland spinning wheel: a traditional design

types of equipment, surrounded by knowledgeable people who are anxious to help. It can also be bewildering to see so many wheels.

However beautiful a wheel, it must work efficiently.

Considerations in choosing a wheel

Comfort It is important that one should feel comfortable while spinning, so consider the height of the wheel and the

Figure 5.12. Using a vertical wheel in Park High School, Pontefract

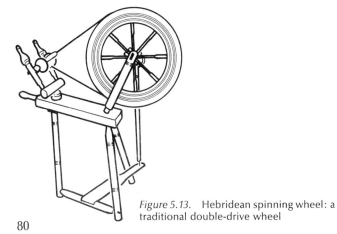

Figure 5.13. Hebridean spinning wheel: a traditional double-drive wheel

Figure 5.14. (a) Louët kit-wheel, manufactured in Holland. (b) Wool-winder on wheel

81

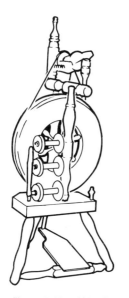 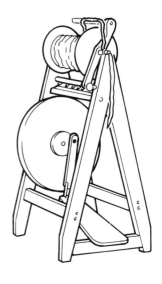

Figure 5.15. 'Wee Peggy' a New Zealand spinning-wheel based on the Shetland pattern

Figure 5.16. The Ashford Indian spinner, suitable for very bulky yarns

sort of chair that is going to be used. Can the treadle be reached easily? Can the wheel be turned without difficulty when starting?

Size and weight Wheels vary greatly in their size. How much space can the wheel be allowed in your home? If the wheel is going to be moved from place to place, it should be fairly light. Will it fit into the boot of the car without damage?

Type There are many makes of wheels, and new models are often introduced. Some of the more popular types are illustrated. It does not follow that the more complicated the wheel is, the better it is going to work.

Ratio If speed is going to be important, it will be necessary to consider the ratio of the wheel to the bobbin, which has an important effect on twist and speed of working. (Large ratios allow higher speeds.)

Driving-band With a double driving-band, beginners can have difficulties if it keeps falling off.

Orifice The diameter of the orifice is something to consider, for a narrow orifice can limit the types of threads which can be spun. If fine threads only are to be spun, a narrow orifice will be satisfactory, but with a wider opening there is scope for both thick and thin threads to be spun. (An Ashford has an orifice measuring 10mm; the de luxe model has an orifice of 16mm diameter.)

Horizontal or vertical The wheel can be in a horizontal or vertical position. In the vertical position, the wheel will take up less room, but usually treadling has to be quicker because the wheel is comparatively small. This can make production slower.

Sewing machine adaptations
During the second world war, spinning units attached to treadle sewing machines were popular. The spinning unit, placed where the machine would have been, was driven by the treadle and band or, later, by a foot-controlled electric motor. Such units can be used for the production of thick yarns very quickly and in large amounts.

Second-hand wheels
It is possible to buy antique spinning-wheels, but if a good sound working wheel is required, be very wary of these. They may look attractive, but you must try using them first. Some have many parts missing and can be very frail. They may have been used in the past, or they may have been made just for decoration. However, you may be lucky and find a well-cared for working wheel.

Sometimes a second-hand spinning-wheel is being sold cheaply because there are some parts missing. Do not buy one without a bobbin and flyer. However, if you are a competent woodworker or know someone who is, it is possible to obtain a bargain. The flyer needs to be well made and to be just right for a particular wheel. The spindle shaft must be straight. Check the sides of the bobbin and spindle whorls.

The wheel itself may be damaged. If there are missing spokes, they should be replaced; make sure the replacements are of similar weight to the others. Check the rim, the joints, and the hub. If the wheel does not run true and has a wobble, it will be extremely irritating.

The maidens, which support the flyer, should fit firmly into the crossbar. The leathers can be replaced if necessary.

The mother-of-all must be in good condition.

Make sure the wheel can stand firmly and evenly on its legs. The treadle and bar would not be difficult to replace. If a footman has to be replaced, make sure the replacement is the right length so that the treadle does not touch the floor. It is not necessary to have a distaff. There is probably a tension screw; check that it will turn and move the mother-of-all backwards and forwards. If there is woodworm, treat it with appropriate chemicals.

Home-made wheels

If you are able to make your own wheel, this would be a very good idea. Patterns are available, but there are certain snags. Try to get a thorough understanding of what makes a good working wheel, and remember that a wheel must not only look beautiful but must work efficiently. The wheel must turn freely, the grooves in the whorls must be just right, and the driving-band must fit satisfactorily into the appropriate places.

A bicycle wheel has more than once proved to be a good starting point for making a spinning-wheel.

6

Using the spinning-wheel

Spinning woollen yarn

A woollen yarn should be soft and airy. Control of the wheel is important, so practise, and take every opportunity to watch demonstrations and talk to experienced spinners.

Start by preparing well-made rolags (Chapter 4). Tie a starter thread to the bobbin leaving at least 12 in hanging out of the orifice (*Figure 6.2*).

Hold the rolag in the right hand. Draw out a few fibres from the rolag and hold them against the starter yarn with plenty of

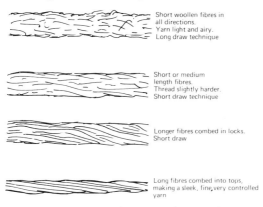

Short woollen fibres in
all directions.
Yarn light and airy.
Long draw technique

Short or medium
length fibres.
Thread slightly harder.
Short draw technique

Longer fibres combed in locks.
Short draw

Long fibres combed into tops,
making a sleek, fine very controlled
yarn

Figure 6.1. Four types of yarn spun from wool. From top to bottom: woollen, semi-wollen, semi-worsted, and worsted

overlap. Treadle slowly and watch the twist travel up. Hold back the thread and stop it winding on, while treadling and building up twist. It is worth practising joining until it can be done very easily.

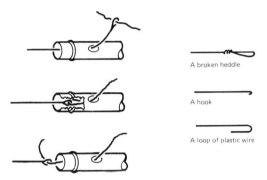

A broken heddle

A hook

A loop of plastic wire

Figure 6.2. Threading the orifice

Figure 6.3. Joining fibres to starter yarn

The method of spinning the rolag will result in a woollen or semi-woollen thread. If a spindle has been used, it is likely that the short draw will come easier than the long draw.

Short draw means that the fibres are drafted for a short distance (3 in to 4 in), and the spin is allowed to travel up. The resulting thread will tend to feel hard, unless the hands move quickly.

The long draw (see next page) involves being able to do the following: to control the spin with the left finger and thumb; to judge when the right amount of twist has built up between orifice and left hand; to take the right arm back for up to a yard, drawing out the fibres at the same time; to pinch with the left finger and thumb but letting a little twist out when it is needed to give strength; and to treadle at the same time, so that the twist can travel as soon as it is allowed to.

Perhaps it is not surprising that so many spinners, especially those who have taught themselves from books, spin with a short draw.

Choose the method that suits the yarn and the purpose for which it is intended. Success is more likely if the following points are followed.

Try to choose a good fleece. Tease the wool carefully and make smooth rolags (not too large). Oil the wool before carding. Make sure the wheel has been oiled. Sit comfortably and check that the driving-band tension has not altered since the last time the wheel was used. Make a good join on to the starter yarn.

Spinning with the long draw
Having joined the rolag to the starter thread, grip the join with the left finger and thumb about 2 in from the rolag juncture (*Figure 6.4*). The right hand holds the rolag lightly,

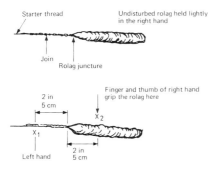

Figure 6.4. Starting to spin with the long draw

but the right finger and thumb should take hold of the rolag firmly about 2 in away from the rolag juncture. Those two inches of rolag will be the part which is to make the yarn. Do not let any more of the rolag slip through the fingers.

Treadle regularly to build up twist between orifice and left hand (*Figure 6.5*).

Keep hold of the rolag and move the right arm to the right.

When the twist has built up, the right arm stretches those 2 in of rolag; at the same time, the left finger and thumb allow twist to come through, the amount of twist depending on how much is wanted and when it is wanted.

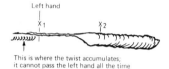

Left hand

X$_1$ X$_2$

This is where the twist accumulates;
it cannot pass the left hand all the time
the left finger and thumb nip the fibres

Figure 6.5. Twist accumulating

As the twist runs into the drafting zone, it should be possible to feel a pull on the yarn. This is made by the left finger and thumb opening and closing when controlling the twist. Do not stop treadling throughout. When the yarn has been spun, leave go with the left hand; the right hand then allows the thread to wind on, stopping a comfortable distance from the orifice (*Figure 6.6*). A little additional twist will be added to the thread as it is wound on.

Each time a new rolag is required, join it carefully, and move the spun thread on to another guide hook.

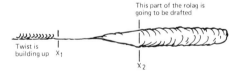

This part of the rolag is
going to be drafted

Twist is
building up   X$_1$

X$_2$

X$_1$ X$_2$

The twist should be allowed to come
through gradually while the fibres
are being drawn out

While it is at this stage the fibres
can be stretched to the appropriate
size of the desired thread.
Feel the pull of the twist as it travels
making the yarn feel like elastic.

Figure 6.6. Stretching the arm

Spinning semi-woollen yarn

This type of yarn is spun with a short draw.

Join the rolag to the starter yarn. Treadle rhythmically and pull the fibres from the rolag fairly quickly; the drafting zone will be fairly short, about 4 in. The left forefinger and thumb hold the thread and stop the twist from travelling up until the right hand has drafted a length for spinning. When the twist has travelled up as far as the end of the drafting zone, the left hand should be ready to move up and stop the twist again. Rhythmical treadling is continuous, and the spun yarn is allowed to wind on the bobbin as spinning continues.

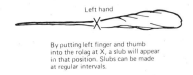

Left hand

By putting left finger and thumb into the rolag at X, a slub will appear in that position. Slubs can be made at regular intervals.

Figure 6.7. Making slubs

The length of draw, the thickness of the fibres, the speed of treadling, and the size of wheel all affect the type of yarn which will be spun. It could be fine and tightly spun, of medium thickness and loosely spun, thick and thin alternately, or a yarn with slubs. (Slubs – unspun lumps – can be made at regular intervals by placing the left finger and thumb into the rolag instead of at the top of the spun yarn when drafting – see *Figure 6.7.*)

Spinning semi-worsted yarn

For a semi-worsted yarn, the fibres can be spun from combed locks of wool. The worsted thread has to be sleek and smooth, so long, lustrous wools are the first choice.

Hold the fibres from one lock of wool in the right hand and join them on to the starter yarn. Keep the fibres parallel and

draw the right hand away from the left. These fibres will form
a fan shape (*Figure 6.8*). As the left hand allows the twist to
travel up, watch the twist and be ready to nip the thread and
draw out the next fibres.

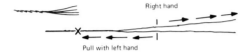

Figure 6.8. Fibres forming a fan shape

The work of the left hand varies; sometimes it just moves
up and controls the spin, occasionally it needs to pull a little
against the right hand. Its main work is to control the twist
which is passing into the drafting zone. The left hand may
need to untwist the thread slightly if it has become too thick
or overtwisted. This is done by a kind of rolling movement
(*Figure 6.9*).

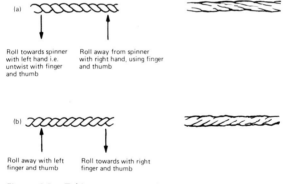

Figure 6.9. Taking out extra twist. (a) Z twist. (b) S twist

As a worsted thread is usually plied, the thread should be
given more twist than a singles woollen because some of the
original twist will be removed in plying.

90

Spinning worsted yarn

If a true worsted thread is required, each process must be carried out with very great care. Stages in the preparation include selective sorting, scouring and drying, choosing the locks, oiling, and combing.

Figure 6.10. Hand wool-combing in late 18th century (photo, Bankfield Museum, Halifax)

Slivers of combed yarn (*Figure 6.11*) are made into rovings by giving them a slight twist, using a long spindle or a great wheel. (There must be insufficient strength in the roving to support a spindle.) Rovings can be wound into loose balls for spinning.

Figure 6.11. Combed fibres

When spinning, the rovings can be held in the left or right hand: try using the left hand first. The instructions will be for the left hand.

The following method of making a smooth worsted thread can be used when spinning tops of any kind, including synthetic fibres. Wool can be bought in top form, either white or coloured.

Join the roving to the starter yarn and pull the fibres out, as shown in *Figure 6.12*.

If spinning fibres which have been made into tops by machinery, take about 24 in and break them away from the roving. Then separate off narrow strips which are a little wider than the required yarn (*Figure 6.13*).

Pull the hands apart gently, and the fibres will separate. Do not hold the hands close together when trying to separate the fibres.

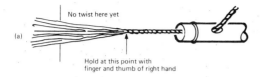

(a)

No twist here yet

Hold at this point with
finger and thumb of right hand

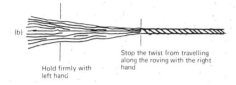

(b)

Stop the twist from travelling
along the roving with the right
hand

Hold firmly with
left hand

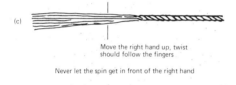

(c)

Move the right hand up, twist
should follow the fingers

Never let the spin get in front of the right hand

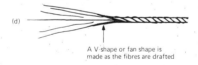

(d)

A V-shape or fan shape is
made as the fibres are drafted

Figure 6.12. Spinning combed fibres

Skeining

When the bobbin is full, the yarn can be removed without taking the bobbin off the spindle shaft. Slip the driving-band from the bobbin whorl over the spindle whorl and slacken the tension. Make sure the yarn winds off freely without catching the arms of the flyer. It can be wound on a

93

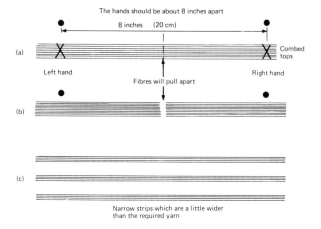

The hands should be about 8 inches apart

8 inches (20 cm)

(a)

Left hand

Combed tops

Right hand

Fibres will pull apart

(b)

(c)

Narrow strips which are a little wider than the required yarn

Figure 6.13. Dividing machine-combed tops

niddy-noddy, around posts, or on a wheel or a floor-rice. If the yarn needs setting, after the skein has been washed, suspend it on a line with a weight attached to the bottom of it. A plastic bottle with water in it is quite good for this because the weight is easily adjustable (*Figure 6.14*).

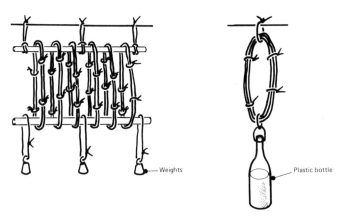

Weights

Plastic bottle

Figure 6.14. Drying skeins

94

Difficulties

The beginner is likely to encounter the following problems.

Yarn disappearing into the orifice This happens to all beginners. It results from undertwisting (*Figure 6.16*). Avoid it by overspinning on purpose, in order to see how the yarn can be controlled before being wound on. Hold on to the yarn and treadle, but do not let the yarn wind on. An overtwisted yarn will be spun. Let it twist back on itself. *Figure 6.15* shows what happens to the overtwisted thread when the tension is released.

When the tension is released this is what happens
to the over twisted thread

Figure 6.15. Over-twisted thread

Uneven, underspun, likely to break or get
tangled on the guide hooks

Figure 6.16. Uneven and underspun thread

Yarn refusing to wind on The driving-band might be too slack because it has stretched: tighten the tension screw, or re-tie or re-sew the band.

If the yarn is uneven, thick slubs may be catching on the guide hooks.

The yarn may be too thick to go through the orifice.

The yarn may have jumped off the guide hooks during irregular treadling, and wound itself over the shaft between the bobbin and the flyer.

The driving-band might not be in the right place.

Wheel reversing This is probably caused by irregular treadling and not keeping the foot flat on the pedal. Check that the

95

wheel has been well oiled, that it is correctly aligned, and that it is firmly fixed in its supports.

Rolag disintegrating   This will happen if there is insufficient twist coming up into the drafting zone. It is a very common occurrence and can be caused by the left finger and thumb holding on too long without allowing twist to come through, or too short a length being drafted. On the other hand, the fault might be in the carding and the making of the rolag. Perhaps the wool was unevenly spread on the carders or perhaps wools of various lengths of staple were carded together.

Uneven yarn   If the yarn is uneven and lumpy, it is probably because of bad carding. Rolags should be fairly small and compact. Large ones are unwieldy and difficult to handle, though opinions vary about size and even on the need to make rolags at all.

Bad joins   Good joins are essential. Allow about 6 in overlap for woollen (long draw) and at least 1 in for worsted spinning.

7

Vegetable fibres

Bundles of fibres found in plants provide strength for leaves, stems, and roots. They are all based on cellulose and are bound together by natural gums and resins. The usefulness

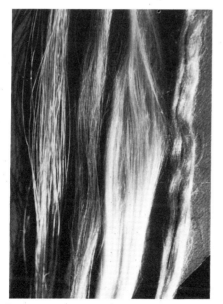

Figure 7.1. A selection of fibres (photo, M. O'Mahoney)

of cellulosic fibres depends on the ease with which the cellulose can be separated from the surrounding materials.

There are three main groups of fibres, classified according to the part of the plant which produces them.

Bast or stem fibres These form the fibrous bundles in the inner bark of the stems of dicotyledonous plants: jute, flax, hemp, sunn, kenaf, urena, ramie, nettle.

Leaf fibres These run lengthwise through the leaves of monocotyledonous plants: sisal, abaca, henequen, cantala, palm, *Phormium tenax*.

Fibres of seeds and fruits Cotton, coir, tree cotton, java kapok, balsa fibre, kumbi.

Flax

Flax was probably the first plant fibre to be used by man for making textiles. Spinning and weaving of flax are mentioned in the Bible, and linen mummy cloths have been identified as more than 4500 years old.

Flax has to go through a large number of processes to free the fibres from the core and the outside straw: before the fibres can be spun, they have to be rippled, retted, grassed,

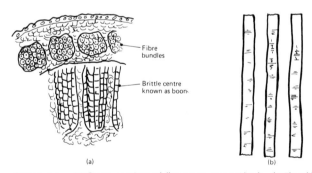

Figure 7.2. (a) Cross-section of flax stem (magnified). (b) Flax fibres seen under a microscope, showing transverse dislocation marks

broken, scutched and hackled. So many spinners start from the stage when this has all been done for them.

Short, broken fibres that remain in the combs used for hackling are called 'tow flax'; the long, lustrous fibres are called 'line'. Bundles of line flax are called 'stricks' or 'heads'. The majority of spinners who spin flax start at this stage. Line can also be used for finger spinning, plaiting, wrapping, and other experiments.

Spinning flax on the spindle
Flax can be spun on the spindle, particularly tow. This can be helpful, because one has to get used to a completely diffe- rent feeling from that of wool. Flax is not as easy to handle as wool, as it does not have the elasticity or the clinging qualities of the latter and fibres will slide past each other.

The first big difference from wool is that flax needs to be spun in a damp state. Have a little bowl of water or a saturated sponge near at hand, so that the right finger and thumb can always be kept slightly wet while spinning. Jelly or carrageen moss can also be used (a spoonful of carrageen moss is boiled in water).

To make a yarn on the spindle, hold the fibres in the left hand, as if spinning with fleece. Wet the right finger and thumb, and draw out a few fibres. Twist these to the leader on the spindle. Draw down a few fibres, allowing spin to run up. While the twist is running up, smooth the fibres upward with the right finger and thumb.

The left hand has to learn to open and close at the right time, just allowing the right amount of fibre to come out and receive the twist. (The fibres in the left hand will become tangled; that is why the shorter fibres should be used for this experiment.) The right hand has to keep the spindle turning, draw down the fibres, and smooth them upwards.

The yarn should be kept smooth, so always work with a wet thumb and finger while stroking it.

Flax is usually S-twisted because of the way the fibres grow.

Before starting to use the spinning-wheel with flax, try spinning on the spindle with the hands reversed: hold the flax in the right hand and draw down with the left. Also turn the spindle to the left (for S twist).

After spinning a reasonable amount, which will probably consist of different thicknesses and irregular twists, make it into a skein.

Wheel-spinning

Preparing the distaff Preparation of the distaff is the first step in spinning flax on the wheel. If a fine, even linen thread is to be achieved, there are certain instructions which should be carried out very carefully to ensure that the fibres are arranged so that they can be pulled out without tangling the rest.

The equipment required consists of a strick of flax, a length of ribbon, an apron or cloth to protect one's lap or table, and a distaff (home-made or on the wheel).

Once you start to prepare the flax, avoid being disturbed.

There are various ways of dressing the distaff. The strick can be held at the top, tied tightly, and attached to the distaff – which must be a tall one. The fibres can be loosely separated and spread out around the pole, and then the straggly ends are tucked up along the bottom. A ribbon is crisscrossed around the fibres. This method makes spinning possible, but it makes drawing out the fibres more difficult than with a cross-combed distaff.

Cross-comb flax as follows.

1. Shake out a strick of flax.
2. Weigh it, and separate off about 1½oz by parting some fibres and pulling away sharply.
3. Tie these fibres with the ribbon about 3in from the top.
4. Sit in an upright chair, cover the lap with a cloth or apron, and tie the ribbon holding the flax round your waist so that the strick hangs straight down.
5. Take the flax in the left hand, as near the end as possible.
6. Keeping the left arm stretched out, move the left arm over to the right knee.
7. The right hand separates a few fibres from the strick and holds them on the right knee with the flat of the hand.

Figure 7.3. Making a filmy crosswise shape. (a) Left hand moving from left to right knee. (b) Left hand moving away from right hand

8. Move the left hand back towards the left knee, keeping the arm outstretched. As this movement takes place, a thin film of fibres should pull across your lap.
9. While moving the left arm towards the left knee, place the palm of the right hand flat on the spreading fibres.

This may need to be done once or twice to help spread them evenly. Do not allow a thick lump of fibres to leave the strick; they must be taken very slowly and gradually.

The purpose of this process is to pull the fibres out into a light, filmy, crosswise shape. They must not lie in a straight line radiating from where the strick is tied.

10. When the left arm has reached the left knee, place the palm of the right hand on these fibres, and raise the left arm a little, thus drawing out a few more fibres.

11. Change hands now. Stretch out the right arm, hold the flax in the right hand, and place the palm of the left hand on the fibres which are on the left knee.

12. The outstretched right arm moves to the right knee, and the left palm helps to spread the fibres.

13. When the right arm reaches the right knee, place the palm of the left hand on the fibres on the knee, and raise the right arm to draw out more fibres.

14. Change the flax into the left hand, and you are ready to start again from 5.

These processes must be continued until all the flax has been spread.

Each layer of flax should be light and filmy and there should be no radiating lines. There should be a continuous fine web of flax folded in a fan shape.

Figure 7.4. A fine web of flax folded in a fan shape

Continuing to use the utmost care, untie the ribbon from around the waist and lift the filmy fan of fibres on to a smooth table. Turn the ends of the fibres up so that straggling loose fibres are tucked in and the bottom of the fan is neat.

Place the distaff on the right-hand edge of the fan, with its top near the knot of ribbon. Roll the distaff across the fan so that the fibres cling to each other. While doing so, keep the top of the distaff and the top of the fan together, building up a cone shape.

Pat the last part of the fan against the fibres and tuck up any straggling ends. Take the ribbon, make sure it is tied securely round the top of the distaff, cross it, and tie it in a bow at the bottom.

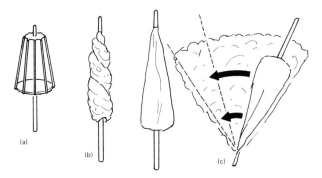

(a)

(b)

(c)

Figure 7.5. (a) A lantern distaff. (b) A stick distaff padded with tissue paper to make a cone shape. (c) Rolling the distaff across the fibres

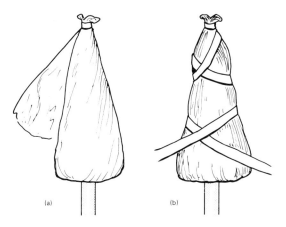

(a)

(b)

Figure 7.6. (a) Distaff almost dressed. (b) Arranging the ribbon

Spinning As flax requires moisture, have a small bowl of water or a wet sponge ready for damping your hand. This can be placed on a stool unless the wheel has a built-in water pot.

Place the distaff to the left of the orifice.

Before joining the flax to the leader, practise treadling, turning the wheel to the left as the flax is to be spun with an S twist.

Take the thread which has been tied to the bobbin and taken through the orifice, and dampen it between finger and thumb. Lay it at an angle across the flax.

Start the wheel turning slowly. With the wetted finger and thumb of the left hand, roll the leader thread gently backwards and forwards until it collects a few fibres from the

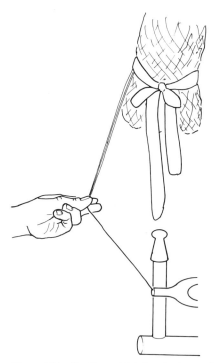

Figure 7.7. Position of left hand when spinning

104

prepared flax. As soon as this happens, draw downwards towards the orifice, letting the leader pull a few fibres.

While getting used to spinning flax, treadle slowly and keep the tension of the driving-band fairly loose so that the movements can be unhurried. Once the different type of drawing and twisting has been mastered, it will not be difficult to spin flax, unless the distaff has been badly dressed. Drafting must be kept even and the supply of overlapping fibres constant.

The following are the left-hand movements.

Wet the thumb. Draw out fibres with thumb and forefinger. Use a slight twisting movement, with the thumb moving towards the tip of the finger. While the thumb is still closed on the finger, allow the hand to be drawn to within 2 in of the orifice. Release the pressure of the thumb slightly.

Roll the yarn between the thumb and the finger as the hand moves to the distaff to draw more fibres down. (It helps to smooth the yarn if it is rolled and twisted.)

Keep the thumb moist, but it is not necessary to dampen it after every draw. When the left hand has to leave go of the fibres to be damped, take over with the right hand.

Up to 12 in at a time can be drawn down, ending about 2 in from the orifice.

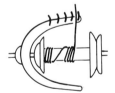

Figure 7.8. Separate lengths on bobbin indicated by diagonal thread

The distaff must be moved round at regular intervals so that the fibres are used evenly. After each turn, the thread should be moved on to another guide hook; move the yarn at frequent intervals to avoid it being built up in one area.

It is very easy to lose the end of the thread, especially if the yarn gets thin and slips through the fingers and the orifice unexpectedly. To make it easier to find a lost end, do not move the thread along the hooks in order, but leave two or three hooks in between (*Figure 7.8*). If the end should get

105

lost, cut the diagonal thread and only one portion of the yarn will be lost. This diagonal thread marks the division between separate lengths.

Continue filling the bobbin in this way so that it becomes evenly full. If too much thread is allowed to build up in one place it slips and becomes loose.

Figure 7.9. If too much thread is allowed to build up in one place it slips and becomes loose

Try to keep all movements rhythmical. When confidence has been gained, tighten the driving-band in order to speed up the spinning and help avoid overspinning.

The ribbon may need to be retied as the flax is spun. At first, the last of the flax on the distaff may be rather muddled, but with practice every bit of flax can be used.

One should aim at getting a very smooth, even thread which is sufficiently twisted to be strong. The type of finished thread will depend on the quality of the flax, the purpose for which it is to be used, the skill of the spinner, and the preparation of the distaff.

If spinning warp threads, use line. Tow is quite suitable for weft, for effect yarns, and for embroidery. The contrast between sleek, smooth threads and rougher uneven threads can be very useful in decorative work.

Possible difficulties When separating the fibres for the distaff, too many fibres may be drawn from the strick at a time. This needs to be done very carefully and patiently. If the fibres are jerked, they could even come away in the hands.

If the fibres will not draw down, they may have been left in thick layers or in straight lines.

The fibres may draw down too freely. This is also caused by a badly dressed distaff.

If the flax drops down low from the distaff, tuck the flax under and start to draw from another position.

If the yarn is hairy remember the following: always draw the fibres down; always smooth the yarn while the twist is running in; always keep the finger and thumb wet; and always smooth towards the distaff and away from the orifice.

If knops or bits of 'boon' (plant waste) appear, pick them out with the right hand; with well-dressed flax, this should not happen.

Very tightly twisted yarn is caused by drawing out the fibres too slowly. With practice, you will learn to judge at what speed to draw out the fibres, how tight to have the driving band, and how quickly to treadle.

If the thread becomes too thick, stop the wheel and twist the thread in the opposite direction by unrolling it with the left hand and pulling it to make it thinner. It is not possible to make it thinner while it is tightly twisted.

If the difficulties are caused by a badly dressed distaff, it is best to start again. Remove the flax, shake it thoroughly, comb it to straighten the fibres and remove short ones, then dress the distaff again.

Finishing processes for linen
Make a skein from the bobbin, tying the ends with care. When adding extra ties, do it as shown in *Figure 7.10* for extra security.

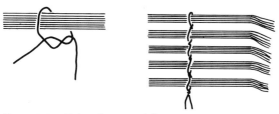

Figure 7.10. Tying skein carefully

The spun linen can be softened by boiling it in soapy water and rubbing it well.

Bleaching The safest way of bleaching yarn is to moisten the skeins and hang them in sunshine. Grass bleaching, as its name suggests, involves placing the skein of yarn or the

107

fabric on grass for several weeks. It is probably the oldest method used and is certainly a safe way of bleaching, even though it can be rather slow. As it is a gentle method it will not damage the fibres. While the flax is on the grass, the colour in the fibre is gradually removed by the oxygen in the atmosphere until in time the linen becomes white. Throughout the process, it should be kept damp and turned over from time to time.

As the original colours of flax vary, the colours after soap and soda bleaching will also vary, so this process could result in deep cream, light fawn, or silvery grey.

Use 1 oz soap and 1 oz of washing soda to 1 gallon of water. Soak the yarn in three parts of the water. Dissolve the soap and soda in the rest of the water.

Lift out the yarn and pour in the solution. Stir well, return the yarn, and bring slowly to the boil. Continue boiling for two hours. Let the yarn cool in the liquid.

If the yarn is not light enough, a fresh solution should be mixed and the process repeated until the right shade is obtained. Leave the yarn lying in the liquid for a day between treatments. Do not use more than four baths altogether.

Household bleaches can safely be used if the directions are carefully observed.

Using handspun linen
Linen threads have a beautiful quality whether bleached or unbleached. Subtle colour changes can be introduced by using different shades of linen, or by making the warp of one shade and the weft of another. If the threads are to be dyed in light colours, bleaching is essential, but it is not so important for dark colours.

Other bast fibres

Jute
Jute has been used since prehistoric times. It probably originated in the Mediterranean area and was taken to India.

Jute can be spun like linen, but it will be harsher and less strong. As the strands may be very long, they can be cut into manageable lengths. The fibres, which are harsh, smooth, lustrous, and inelastic, can be used for many kinds of experiments. Their natural colour is yellow, brown, or dirty grey. They can be dyed and used in lightly twisted ropes or in hangings, or they can be carded and spun. Smooth or rough threads can be made, depending on the methods used for preparation and spinning. Oil added to the fibre makes spinning easier. However, jute threads deteriorate in water, so they are not very durable.

As jute is cheap, reasonably strong, and plentiful, it is mostly used in the manufacture of sacks and packing cloths, but finer qualities are made into curtains and furnishing fabrics and can also be mixed with wool to produce cheap clothing fabrics.

Hemp

It has been recorded that hemp was used in China in 2800 BC. The plant is now cultivated in many European countries, in Asia and in the American continent. The fibre is used throughout the world.

Hemp is a coarser fibre than flax, and it is dark and difficult to bleach. String, cord, and ropes are made from hemp, and in Italy they produce a hemp fabric similar to linen.

As hemp is stronger and softer to use than jute, it is an attractive fibre for the handspinner. It could be spun in the same way as short flax fibres; the addition of a little oil would help to make smooth threads.

Ramie

Ramie is also known as 'China grass' or 'rhea'. The fibre comes from plants which belong to a family of stingless nettles and grow in many countries.

Before spinning ramie fibres, they must be degummed. Repeated soaking or scraping will do this, and soda or lime could be used if available.

Ramie fibre is very attractive, being white and lustrous and looking like linen. It can be as strong as linen and is often used industrially instead of it.

It is not easy to obtain ramie in an unprepared state, so a handspinner will probably start from the roving stage. When spinning a roving, employ a similar action to that used when spinning combed woollen tops, using a V-shaped drafting action. The fibre will feel stronger than cotton but less resilient than wool, so it will have to be spun fairly quickly, taking care not to overspin. Ramie can be blended with other fibres; it has a natural lustre and softness which enhance the final thread or cloth.

Nettle

In Scandinavia, nettles have been cultivated for fibres which have been made into sails. They can be made into twine and rope, and also be woven into canvas.

Stinging nettles can be unpleasant to gather, and a large quantity is required to give a good supply of fibres.

There are other bast fibres which can be found growing wild in most parts of the world. They do not have great commercial value, but the handspinner might find it useful to look around and try to discover local wild plants which could prove very useful.

Leaf fibres

Sisal

Ancient Mexicans and Aztecs clothed themselves in fabrics woven from sisal. It is obtained from the plant *Agave sisalana* which grows in Central America and elsewhere. Huge, firm, fleshy leaves form a rosette on a short trunk. When the plants are about four years old, the leaves are harvested, the pulpy matter is scraped from the fibres, and the fibre is hung up to dry and bleach in the sun after washing.

Sisal is one of the most valuable of cordage fibres, used for making baler and binder twine. It is very strong, lustrous and of a good creamy-white colour. Polish weavers have used vast quantities of sisal with great skill in wall hangings, both in its natural colour and in glowing colours.

As sisal fibres are tough and fairly unyielding, they are not easy to spin. That is probably why they are often manipulated and twisted in the hands rather than spun on a spindle or wheel. If a thick, strong yarn is required, it would probably be best to spin sisal like flax, but it would be quite hard on the hands, and hard on the wheel if it was not a strong one.

Direct cotton and acid dyestuffs give attractive shades on sisal with good light fastness.

Phormium tenax

Phormium tenax is the 'flax' which is indigenous to New Zealand. Unlike flax (*Linum usitatissimum*), which is a bast fibre, *Phormium tenax* is a leaf fibre. The plant has a fan-like appearance and grows to a height of 8 ft to 10 ft. The fibres lie longitudinally in the leaf, which has a very high fibre content. They were used in the ropemaking industry.

Molly Duncan's book *Creative Crafts with Wool and Flax* contains much useful information on using this flax. She finds it easier to spin *Phormium* on the jumbo spinner because of the larger hooks on the flyer; the drop spindle is also recommended. A jumbo flyer unit is an accessory which can be fitted to an Ashford wheel in order to spin soft bulky yarns. Molly Duncan always dampens her fingers when spinning any kind of flax; some spinners prefer to use linseed oil. For general weaving, she uses the fibres without spinning because they are long enough for weft threads, and the short tow is blended with wool for textured effects.

Cotton

Cotton is not an easy fibre to spin, as the staple is usually very short and the fibres slip past each other very quickly. But there are wonderful examples of superb spinning in the form of exquisite cottons and muslins. These delicate threads were spun on primitive spindles, sometimes just a stick or twig, by Egyptians and Indians.

We know that cotton fabrics were made by the ancient Egyptians and by the earliest of Chinese civilisations. In Peru, specimens of woven cotton fabric have been found in desert tombs, and in India, beautiful cotton fabrics were being produced in 1500 BC.

Cotton grows on a plant which reaches 4 ft to 6 ft in height. Creamy white flowers wither and die, leaving small green seedpods or 'bolls'. When the boll opens, it reveals a mass of

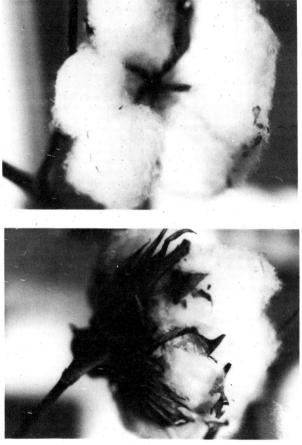

Figure 7.11. Cotton bolls

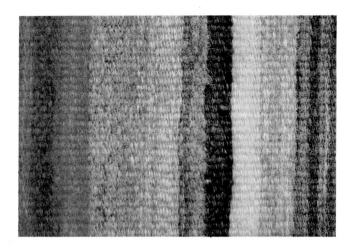

Natural dyed hand-spun, hand-woven material for a chair seat by Karin Plough

Different materials
dyed with indigo

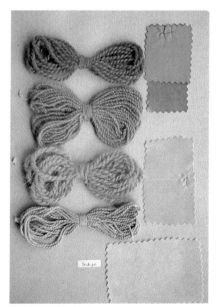

Above. Fleece, spun wool and cotton dyed with woad

Below. Fleece, spun wool, cotton, raffia, cotton and silk dyed with onion skins. Four mordants were used to obtain these colours

fine hairs, varying in colour from white to pale brown and in length from ⅜in to 2in. The moisture evaporates from the fibres and the cell walls collapse. When seen under the microscope, the fibres form ribbon-like structures which are flat and twisted, rather like barley sugar. Inside the boll, the fibres are tightly packed into distorted positions, but when they dry out in the air, they twist lengthwise; these twists can be left-handed or right-handed. An average fibre will have 125 twists to an inch.

The boll contains less than half its weight of cotton. The fibres are detached from the seeds by a machine called a 'gin'; ginned cotton is called 'lint'. An inner coating of hairs is firmly attached to the seed. They are too short to be spun but as 'cotton linters' form a source of raw material for the manufacture of rayon.

Before cotton is ready for spinning, it has several more stages to go through. It is cleaned by machines until it is left in the form of an enormous roll of cotton wool, called a 'lap'. Then it is carded, and in this process most of the remaining impurities and short fibres are removed. The carded cotton forms loose ropes which can just cling together. These are stretched and drawn several times until they form narrow slivers with well-arranged, uniform fibres.

Figure 7.12. Cotton fibres seen under a microscope

Narrow slivers ready for spinning are called 'rovings'. The rovings are given a slight twist to prevent them from breaking or disintegrating. Handspinners sometimes use rovings for spinning on their wheels, but the resulting thread does not

113

have the texture and quality of a handspun cotton which has been prepared by hand from the boll.

Preparing cotton
Take a cotton boll, pull the fibres away from the seeds, and try not to rearrange the fibres, for if they remain fluffy they can be spun straight away. It is possible to make the fibres fluffier by whipping them up with a flexible twig.

Figure 7.13. Pull fibres *away* from the seed

For carding, if possible use extra fine close-set carding cloth, and keep the carders for cotton. Place a small handful of whipped cotton across the carders and card it carefully with light brushing strokes. The cotton should make a fairly dense rolag. It can be rolled on the back of the carder or it can be rolled sideways along the carder.

Spinning on a spindle
There are many ways of spinning cotton on a spindle, but the most usual way is to use a supported spindle. The short, smooth fibres are not as easy to deal with as wool, as they will not support the weight of the spindle while the twist is running in. On the other hand, if the thread is over-twisted, it will be strong enough to hold the spindle, but the result will not be satisfactory – unless a thick, curly thread is specially required for decorative purposes.

Prepare the spindle in the usual way. If possible, choose one with a lightweight whorl. Place a shallow bowl or saucer on a stool at a convenient height, so that the spindle can be supported during spinning. Take some of the fluffy fibres in the left hand, and pull a few away to make the join on the starting yarn. Twist the spindle in a clockwise direction with the right hand. The finger and thumb of the left hand should

Figure 7.14. Suspend spindle over a bowl or saucer

be slightly open as they draw out the fibres in an upward movement. The right hand should be ready to control the twist as it travels upwards.

As the spindle is supported in the dish, the thread does not have to bear the weight of the spindle.

At first, the length of draw will of necessity be short because the fibres feel so different from the familiar clinging handle of wool. Practise using the spindle in this way until it is possible to control the spin and make it travel for a longer distance.

There are times when it is useful to use the thumb and first finger of the left hand to untwist the fibres slightly in order to allow the thread to be spun evenly.

Try to understand what is happening and, without twisting the spindle, use the hands to check. For example, if the cotton in the hand is difficult to pull out, stop spinning and examine the fibres. The twist has probably travelled too far ahead.

After using teased cotton and getting used to the handle of the fibres, try spinning with a rolag. This may feel easier, and it is quite possible that the long-draw method can be used. If the long draw is used, the thread will be softer and very suitable for wefts. (Thread spun with a short draw will be firmer, harder, and stronger. It could be used for a warp, but a two-ply yarn might be safer.)

Wheel-spinning

After spindle-spinning cotton, the handle of the smooth fibres will be familiar, so spinning on the wheel will be a question of adjusting the rate of treadling and the speed of winding-on.

Alter the tension by loosening the driving band so that the spun thread winds on fairly slowly, and before starting to spin, practise treadling slowly and rhythmically. This should help to produce a thread which is over-twisted, but it will be much easier to deal with such a thread than with one which is undertwisted. If the thread keeps breaking or pulling apart because it is drawn into the orifice too quickly, it will be difficult to find the end, but a strong, overtwisted thread gives one the opportunity to get things right gradually.

Figure 7.15.   Fibres in a fan shape

To start with, hold both hands near the orifice and draw out the fibres in a fan shape. Remember that it might be helpful to use the slight untwisting movement with the left hand.

Try eventually to spin a smooth, strong yarn that is not overtwisted.

8

Animal hair

Dog hair

Dog hair is a very popular fibre with many people. Although the physical structure of hair is different from that of wool, the soft undercoats of some dogs are similar to fine wool fibres. They have a slightly soapy feel, rather like angora rabbit fur.

If dogs are well cared for, their hair will be pleasant to use, and not matted or dirty. The hair should not be cut, but combed out and collected when the dog moults, once or twice a year.

If the dog has a double coat, like the corgi, use only the undercoat. It is always shed first and is several shades lighter than the top coat. As the undercoat is very fine and short, it is easier to spin if blended with a little fine sheep's wool. Longer hair from such breeds as the Samoyed, Keeshund, and Afghan can be spun without any preparation and does not need additional sheep's wool.

Carding
As colour, texture, and length vary, it is best to card the hair if an even thread is required. On the other hand, the thread may be more attractive if the colours are used without too much blending.

Spinning

Proceed as for wool, but put plenty of twist in the yarn. Some of the short fibres may rub off, but the yarn is beautifully soft and fluffy.

Uses

There are endless possibilities for weaving. Soft yarns can be produced for stoles and scarves, and firmer threads can be made into suit and coat lengths. Yarn can be used singly or plied. Mixture yarns can be made by plying dog hair with fine threads of other materials. Fancy-spun threads may also be designed by experimenting with different colours, twists, and materials.

Jerseys, hats, gloves and scarves can be knitted from the yarn.

Washing

Wash spun dog hair carefully, like woollens. It does not shrink but some of the very fine fibres have a tendency to felt if not handled carefully.

Rabbit hair

Angora rabbits may be white, cream, fawn, grey, black, or variegated in colour. The hair dyes well, so white Angora is particularly popular. The average length of staple is 3 in to 5 in, but it can vary from ½ in to 7 in or 8 in. Rabbits between the age of five and 18 months are said to provide the best wool for spinning fine, soft yarns.

Sorting

The fur should be carefully sorted if one wishes to spin threads of the very highest quality. The back and shoulders provide the longest staple, and coarse hairs are found towards the tail. If a very even thread or material is required, long hairs should be pulled out and not mixed with the soft fur because they spoil the yarn and fabric. They do not dye so easily, and they shed. However, if the design needs irregular dyeing and long fibres, they should be left in.

118

Store the different sorts in separate boxes, placing layers of fur in an airtight, paper-lined tin with a layer of paper between each layer of fur.

Spinning

Spinning angora rabbit fur can be very challenging. A beautiful thread can be spun, but because the fibres are smooth and slippery, they are quite difficult to control. If the fur has been packed in layers, it should be ready for spinning without any other preparation. When spinning on the wheel, use the hands as if spinning combed wool for a worsted thread. Adjust the driving band so that it is fairly slack at first. The twist will be increased, but this will help the spinner to get accustomed to the handle of the fibre. Start by spinning the coarser fibres at first.

A light hand spindle could be used; or if the whorl is heavy, support the spindle in a bowl.

Use a hand-spun woollen starter yarn. It is easier to join the angora fibres on to it if the thumb is wet. When joining the yarn after a break, always untwist the fibres of the thread to enable the new fibres to cling.

It is difficult to judge the amount of twist required for short, smooth fibres. Start by making a hard-twisted thread by having a fairly slack driving-band, then tighten the band and spin an almost untwisted thread, like a roving. Between these two will be the happy medium, achieved by the right tension on the driving-band and the correct speed of drafting. The object is a strong, soft yarn.

When spinning the very short fibres, the hand movements must be very quick, because only a small amount can be drawn out at a time. If fibres are less than an inch in length, they could be mixed on the carders with Down wool.

Camel hair

Every camel yields about 5 lb of hair every year, shed in matted locks. The outer coat consists of tough hairs which may reach 12 in; underneath is a downy coat of fine, soft hair

1 in to 6 in long. This soft hair, the most valuable part of the fleece, feels as soft and fine as Merino wool.

There is a great difference between the outer and inner coat, so the term 'camel hair' could mean long, strong fibres

Figure 8.1. Fine and coarse camel hairs, both magnified ×180

or delicate, soft fibres. Each type requires its own kind of handling and will produce quite different yarns. When ordering camel hair from a supplier, study the samples so that the correct quality is obtained.

Preparation
If camel hair has not been treated at all, it may need careful washing before being carded.

In roving form, it can be spun as for worsted, but in order to retain the soft character of the fibre, the driving-band should be moderately tensioned so that there is no danger of over-spinning. (If the driving-band is too slack, there will be too much spin in the thread and it will become tightly twisted and feel hard.)

Camel undercoat is a very rewarding fibre to use, on its own or blended with Merino or fine Down fleece, but it takes delicate handling.

Cashmere

Cashmere comes from the Kashmir or Tibetan goat, which is to be found in parts of Asia Minor, north India, and China. It has long, coarse hair on the outside, and fine, soft down next to the body. In the spring, the downy cashmere fibre is combed from the fleece, keeping it as separate as possible

120

from the coarse hair. Only about 4 oz of true cashmere fibre is obtained from each animal.

Downy fibres are 1 in to 3½ in long, and the coarser hairs 2 in to 5 in long. They are grey, buff-coloured, or white. The finest fibres are finer than Merino wool. Cashmere makes warm, comfortable fabrics which drape beautifully.

The term 'cashmere' has sometimes been incorrectly used to describe fabrics made from fine botany wool.

Spinning
When spinning on the spindle, as the fibres are short and slippery, use a light spindle.

If spinning on a wheel from a roving, hold it loosely in the hand and allow the spun thread to wind on to the bobbin quickly. Try to avoid over-spinning. It will take patience and skill to achieve the right rhythm.

Llama hair

Llamas are to be found in the mountainous regions of Ecuador, Peru, Bolivia, and north-west Argentina. The fleece is a mixture of fine, soft fibres and dull, inelastic, coarse hairs. The natural colours are black, brown, and white. Llama fibres are soft and strong, but the undercoat is not as fine as that of the camel. It is sometimes possible to obtain llama fleece from a zoo.

The fibre can be spun like alpaca. Llama and alpaca fibres can be compared with wool of 55 to 60s quality.

Alpaca hair

The alpaca is closely related to the llama and lives in the same regions of South America. The fleece is beautifully soft, lustrous, and silky, with good elasticity. It averages a yearly growth of 6 in to 8 in, and if not clipped, the fibres can reach a length of 30 in. The alpaca is the most valuable of the fleece-bearing animals of the Andes. Colours of the fleece include black, brown, fawn, and white. Threads spun from alpaca are very soft, fine, strong, and light. Much alpaca is exported in the form of scoured, combed tops.

Figure 8.2. White (left) and pigmented (right) alpaca, magnified

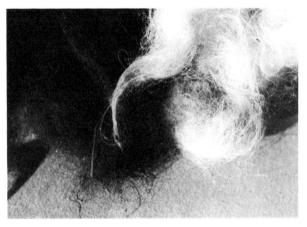

Figure 8.3. Brown and white alpaca (photo, M. O'Mahoney)

If carding alpaca, take the rolag from the carder across the wires so that the worsted method of spinning can be used. If starting from combed tops, hold the fibres firmly to prevent twist from going too far ahead.

Vicuna hair

The vicuna is a small species of llama. It has the rarest wool-like fibre in the world. The natural colours are white, fawn or brown, and the fibres are about 2 in long.

122

In the past, the vicuna had to be shot for its fleece, which weighed about 1 lb. The Peruvian government allowed only a limited number of vicunas to be shot annually, so garments made from vicuna are obviously extremely rare and expensive. It is thought that vicuna fibre will become plentiful if the animal can be domesticated.

Vicuna fibres can be compared with 120s or 130s wool. As 100s is the finest Merino, these numbers suggest a very rare quality.

Mohair

Mohair is the name given to the long, lustrous hair which comes from the angora goat. The countries which provide most of the world's mohair are Turkey, South Africa, and the United States of America.

Figure 8.4. Angora goat

The goats are usually clipped twice a year, and 4 lb to 5 lb is obtained from each animal. The fibres consist of various qualities, and the fleeces are graded into three types: 'tight lock' has ringlets and is fine, 'flat lock' is wavy and of medium quality, and 'fluffy' or 'open' fleece is the least valuable. Mohair, like wool, contains kemp.

Mohair in its natural state contains grease, dirt, and vegetable impurities, which could amount to 30 per cent of the

123

weight of the raw fibre. After scouring, the fibre is white and silky.

An angora kid at the age of six months will provide fibres 4 in to 6 in long; at 12 months, the mohair will have grown to 9 in to 12 in.

Figure 8.5. Symbol of the International Mohair Association

Mohair absorbs water readily and will normally hold as much moisture as wool. The fibre has a smooth handle, so the light is reflected from the surface, thus giving mohair its beautiful lustre. Mohair is a thick, strong fibre, so it is particularly useful when a hard-wearing material is required.

Preparation
If raw mohair has been obtained, it should be thoroughly washed. First soak it in very hot water, then wash it in hot soapy water, then rinse it. Repeat this until you are satisfied with its cleanliness.

Worsted-type threads
When using long-fibre mohair to make into a fine, sleek yarn, sort the fibres into qualities as for wool. Comb the long hairs and place them together to form locks. These locks can be spun by holding them tightly over the fingers of one hand and pulling the fibres away to spin in a semi-worsted way.

Before spinning, spray the fibre with a small amount of water. Do not leave the thread on the spindle, but make a skein and stretch it gently while it is still damp.

Mohair threads can be used to make light stoles, scarves, and cardigans.

Short fibres

Short fibres left over from the combing can be carded and made into a woollen-type yarn with the characteristics of mohair – lightness and softness.

The fibres from mohair kids are also short. They are very soft and silky, but if carded carefully they can be spun into fine, delicate yarns of excellent quality.

A strong, heavy yarn with no resemblance to the threads already described could be spun by using the strong, coarser hairs and making a thicker, tightly spun singles thread, and then plying it.

Dyeing

Acid dyestuffs can be used very successfully on mohair, as it has a great affinity for dyes. Strong coloured threads which have been given a light brushing either before or after weaving make beautiful stoles.

Brushing

After the skein has been made, keep it under tension and brush it with a wet hairbrush. If the brush is not dipped in hot water, the threads will be ruined, but with care the fibres can be raised without causing any disintegration.

Musk-ox hair

Musk-oxen are dark-brown animals somewhere between oxen and sheep in size. They have loose hair hanging from them from nose to tail. The loose hair, measured by length and diameter of fibre, is said to be the finest in the world – finer than cashmere.

The under-wool is collected at the end of April. Bulls yield 6 lb and cows 5 lb. The hair is a darkish grey and extremely soft, so a very gentle, delicate touch is required when spinning.

9

Silk

The silkworm (the caterpillar of the moth *Bombyx mori*) produces silk as a material for webs, cocoons, and 'climbing ropes' when it is about to change into a chrysalis.

Reeling

The thread spun on the cocoon is unwound after immersion in boiling water, which softens the gum coating the fibres.

The largest diameter is at the beginning, where the worm started to spin, and the smallest diameter is at the end. The best grade of silk (organzine) is taken in one unbroken length from the centre of the filaments.

Ten pounds of cocoons are needed for 1 lb of reeled silk. Only perfect cocoons are reeled. Reeled silk is wound into skeins and then made into bundles of about 6 lb for export.

Thrown silk and spun silk

Thrown silk (from the Anglo-Saxon word *thrawan*, to twist) is the very best quality. Some silk is woven after reeling only, but usually two or three of the multi-filament strands are twisted together. If silk is woven from yarn with gum on it, the material will feel stiff and look dull, but after degumming it will be soft and lustrous.

The throwster is able to use about half the silk filaments, so there is quite a large quantity left over. This very valuable 'waste' is made into spun silk. Hand-spinners will be able to use this silk for a variety of silk threads, according to whether they use fibres which have been carded or combed.

Figure 9.1. Finger-twisting silk noils

Silk waste is of the following kinds.

Floss The outer silk which the worm spun to attach itself to the straw on which they live. It is soft, fine, and weak.

Frisson The first strong threads pulled off the cocoon.

Bassinets From damaged cocoons and the last layers of silk spun when the worm was exhausted.

Noils Short fibres left after degumming and combing.

Preparation for spinning

Frisson This will have to be degummed first.

Prepare a solution of hot soapy water. (Use rainwater or soft water throughout if possible.) Simmer the silk in this for about 1½ hours. Do not let it boil, but keep to a temperature of 195°F (90°C).

Rinse thoroughly in hot water, and then repeat the process but use less soap.

It may be necessary to repeat the process a third time if the gum has not been dissolved from the filaments.

If spun silk is to be dyed, save the liquid from the first 'boil off' as it helps to make the dye level.

Before hanging the silk in a warm place and away from direct sunlight to dry, make sure it has been well rinsed.

The silk should be soft, lustrous, and clean, looking quite different from the untidy white fibres which resembled straw. As these filaments are too long to spin, cut them into lengths of 3 in to 4 in, comb them, and spin as for worsted.

The waste left over from this can be used in mixture yarns or can be dyed for blending.

When spinning, remember that the fibres will not cling quite so readily as wool, so at first hold them tightly, use a shorter draw than for wool, and increase the amount of twist by slackening the driveband. This will result in an overspun yarn, but with practice the winding on can be speeded up and a softer thread spun.

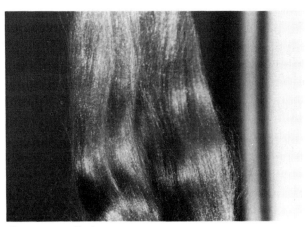

Figure 9.2. Silk sliver

Bassinet If the silk is received in a tangled, degummed state, it can be combed or brushed. These preparations will help to determine the kind of threads to be spun. It will not be possible to spin a sleek yarn, but the resulting thread should be attractively textured. The colour is creamy fawn.

Silk slivers Sometimes silk can be bought in slivers. It will be clean, degummed, and fairly easy to handle.

Wild silk

Wild (tussah) silk may be yellow, brown, grey, or green. It is sturdier, coarser, and not so lustrous as cultivated silk. The subtle shades make it very appealing to handspinners.

Spinning

Silk can be carded gently and, according to the method used, can be brushed so that the fibres are kept parallel as if combed, or rolled into a rolag.

If a drop spindle is used, try supporting it in a bowl. For very fine threads, use a light whorl, but when spinning coarser threads, choose a spindle with a heavier whorl.

When using the spinning-wheel, start with a fairly slack driving band and, after practising and getting used to the handle of silk, gradually increase the tension.

Allow the fibres to come from the right hand in a fan-shape. If there is too much spin, or it goes too far ahead, untwist the thread a little with the left hand and let the spin travel towards the right hand.

Try plying a singles of fine wool and a singles of silk, or mix silk and wool on the carders.

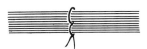

Figure 9.3. Tying skeins securely

Skeining
Make skeins if there is still some gum left in the silk or if the silk is to be dyed. Use a niddy-noddy if possible. Silk needs careful tying because of its slippery nature.

129

10

Manmade fibres

Scientists have made remarkable advances in the development of fibres which can replace, improve, or blend with natural fibres. The term 'manmade' includes regenerated fibres (based on cellulosic raw materials) and synthetic fibres (based on chemically synthesised polymers).

Manmade fibres can now be produced in different forms – as filament yarns, as tow, or as staple fibre. Many confusing names are given to these fibres: they can be known by generic names, brand names, or both. An EEC directive insists that practically all textiles have to be marked with the generic name of the fibre, which is based mainly on its chemical composition.

Many handspinners dislike using synthetic fibres, but we should give them a fair trial, find out what they have to offer and try to make our own new discoveries about them.

Rayon

In 1664, Robert Hooke wrote a book in which he discussed the possibility of converting vegetable matter into silk. Two hundred years later a French chemist, Chardonnet, who was helping Pasteur in his researches into a silkworm disease which was causing great devastation, thought of trying to make an artificial silk. His chemical knowledge made him realise that what he had to do was to take cellulose, which was cheap and plentiful, dissolve it to make a viscous fluid, extrude it through a jet (like the silkworm's spinneret), and solidify the thread. Others were also making experiments, and by the end of the 19th century there were four main processes of manufacture. Of these, the viscose process proved the most successful. Wood pulp provides most of the raw material for viscose rayon.

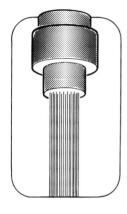

Figure 10.1. A spinneret (British Man-made Fibres Federation)

These first successful manmade fibres were regenerated; that is to say, they were made from a natural fibrous material which was dissolved and then made into a regenerated fibre. Man could therefore make a fibre, but only if he started with a fibre or a fibrous material such as wood-pulp.

The firm of Courtaulds carried on the pioneer work of developing the industry. The first viscose spinning plant was in Coventry. The manufacturing process is as follows.

Large sheets of wood-pulp, made from spruce and looking like blotting paper, arrive at the factory. These are treated with caustic soda solution and shredded so that they look like breadcrumbs. The crumbs are left to age, then carbon disulphide is added. After the addition of dilute caustic soda solution, the mixture is stored for four to five days so that it can ripen or become more viscous. The viscous liquid is filtered several times and air bubbles are removed. Then the liquid is forced through tubes which have nozzles at the ends

131

into a solution of sulphuric acid and salts. A delicate thread appears which is caught, led out of the bath into a hollow container, stretched, and wound up into a cake.

Figure 10.2. Wet spinning

Nylon

In October 1938, news of the first synthetic textile fibre was announced. This was nylon.

Nylon was the result of a chance discovery. Du Pont, one of America's largest chemical firms, gave their research chemists a free hand to explore anything they liked. The team, led by Carothers, chose to study the long-chain molecules of rubbers, plastics, and fibres. Two discoveries were eventually made: a fibre could be spun from molten material, and it could be drawn to change its properties. They then developed a method of spinning by extrusion through jets, like rayon.

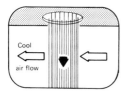

Figure 10.3. Melt spinning

Nylon is a truly synthetic yarn: the primary raw materials are coal or petroleum, air, and water.

Nylon is melt-spun. Nylon chips are made, then they are melted and become a molten mass which is forced through holes in a spinneret. The jets of molten material are cooled and solidified by contact with a stream of cold air. Then the filaments are drawn by passing them round two rollers, the second moving faster than the first. They may become drawn to four times their original length. The filaments become finer, and their dull opaque appearance becomes lustrous and translucent.

The characteristics of the fibre can be controlled during manufacture. At first, it was always made in the form of continuous filament, but after 1945 it was produced as staple fibre as well.

Nylon is not an imitation of a natural material but a new fibre with unique properties. It adds strength, lightness, elasticity, and dimensional stability to other fibres.

Terylene

The discovery of nylon led to the manufacture of many other synthetic fibres. Terylene, the British polyester fibre produced by ICI, was the first one of any real importance. Terylene was a new substance built by chemists from the simplest of raw materials and chemically distinct from nylon. Terylene was discovered in 1941 by Dr J. T. Dickson and J. R. Whinfield.

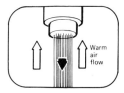

Figure 10.4. Dry spinning

Terylene is produced in a similar way to nylon.

Terylene staple adds fullness and warmth, because entrapped air gives an insulating effect. It is strong, light, and keeps its shape well.

Acrylic fibres

Acrylic fibres are also true synthetics, being mainly produced from a liquid derivative of oil-refining and coal-carbonisation processes. Orlon, the first, was invented by Du Pont in the USA in 1949.

Acrylic fibres are produced in tow and staple form. They can be used in a wide range of fabrics which includes jersey fabric, blankets, carpets, underwear, high-bulked knitted outerwear, and pile fabrics. When blended, they are used with wool in suits and with cotton in shirts, blouses, and dress fabrics.

Fabrics made from acrylics have a warm, cashmere-like handle, and light weight. They are strong, hard-wearing, and non-irritant. Correctly made garments will not shrink or stretch, and they are not attacked by moths or mildew.

Polyolefin fibres

Polypropylene multifilament yarn is made by polymerising propylene gas, a byproduct of oil. The method of producing it commercially was discovered by an Italian.

These multifilament yarns are mainly used for industrial purposes, including ropes, cordage, fishing nets twines, filter cloths, dye bags and webbings.

New developments

Until 1964, all manmade fibres were produced by forcing a liquid chemical through fine holes in a spinneret, but since then some yarns are made by stretching and splitting a film of polypropylene or by extruding a flat tape or ribbon. Polypropylene films are extruded, but the equivalent of the spinneret is a long, narrow slit. The yarns are coarse and firm in handle. They combine lightness with high strength. These yarns are used where sisal, manila, and jute used to be manufactured into strings, twines, and ropes.

Methods of spinning

Natural fibres (e.g. cotton, wool, flax) are spun into yarn by being prepared in various ways and then pulled out and twisted. These fibres may be carded or combed and spun by the woollen or worsted method.

Solution or melt spinning involves making a continuous filament by extruding a solution through fine holes. This is done by the silkworm and spider, by wet spinning (the filaments from the spinneret are extruded into a coagulating bath), by dry spinning (the fibre-forming chemical is dissolved in a volatile solvent which evaporates in warm air), or by melt spinning (the hard polymer is melted, extruded through the spinneret, and cooled in the air).

Having been through a wet spinning, dry spinning, or melt spinning process, many of these continuous filaments will then go through the same spinning process as that used for natural fibres. The filaments will have to be cut up into short lengths and made into staple fibre. This can then be spun on its own or mixed with natural fibres.

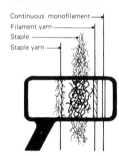

Continuous monofilament
Filament yarn
Staple
Staple yarn

Figure 10.5. Yarns magnified

When spinning natural fibres, the spinner has to select the material and then use skill to produce a yarn of the thickness and texture required for a given cloth. After spinning, the yarn might be dyed, plied, or made into a fancy yarn. But the chemist can control the yarn when manufacturing it, making it lustrous or dull, of any degree of fineness, to any required length of staple, as a coloured filament or staple by 'dyeing' the spinning solution, and in bulked and textured qualities to improve drape and handle.

Ways in which the type of thread can be manipulated or modified during spinning include the following: the thickness of filaments can be affected by the number and size of

135

holes in the spinneret; the filaments can be stretched while in a plastic state; flat filaments can be produced by using long, narrow holes in the spinneret; the diameter of the filament can vary between thick and thin; other substances can be mixed with the fibre-forming material before the filament is extruded: e.g. pigments, dyes, anti-static agents and flame retardant agents.

Fibres can be passed through fluted rollers and become crimped mechanically before being cut up. Crimp can also be created chemically. A good crimp seems to enhance the quality of the yarn. Even straight, coarse wool is sometimes crimped to make better carpets.

Staple fibre

Staple fibre is made by chopping continuous filaments into short lengths. They can be blended with other fibres and also spun by traditional methods in the following ways.

Cotton spinning   This system uses staple lengths from 28 mm to 60 mm.

Worsted spinning   The yarns spun by this system are very regular because 'tops' are used. These contain more parallel fibres of longer staple length, measuring 50 mm to 200 mm.

Woollen spun yarns   These are produced from fibres ranging from 40 mm to 100 mm in length. The fibres are in a more random state, so the resulting thread is more hairy and bulky and less regular than worsted yarns.

High-bulk yarns   The methods already described could be applied to natural fibres, but there is an additional property which can be built in to manmade yarns: 'high bulk'. Staple fibres which have been pre-stretched and relaxed are blended with fibres which have only been pre-stretched.

Generic names

Acetate   A chemical derivative of cellulose. It has silk-like qualities of soft handle and drape.

136

Acrylic   The fibres combine durability with an inherent soft-ness and a wool-like appearance.

Elastane   Based on polyurethane, has high stretch and re-covery.

Modacrylic   Like acrylic with the additional property of flame retardancy.

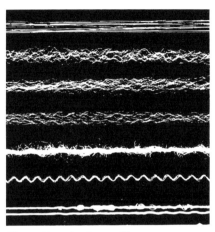

Figure 10.6.   Variety in fibres

Modal   Made from cellulose, is absorbent and retains its strength when wet.

Nylon   Has high strength, abrasion resistance, and ability to recover from stretching, and it can be textured easily.

Polyester   Has good abrasion resistance, resilience, and easy-care properties of minimum ironing and quick drying. It blends very well with natural fibres.

Polyolefin   Describes polyethylene and polypropylene. These fibres have important industrial uses – in fishing gear, ropes and cordage, sacking, and carpet backing.

137

Triacetate   Chemically similar to acetate, has quick drying properties, and is used in hand-knitting yarns and furnishings.

Viscose   Made from cellulose, it was the first man-made fibre. Widely used in a variety of ways.

The British Man-Made Fibres Federation (24 Buckingham Gate, London SW1E 6LB, telephone 01-828 0744) publishes a *Guide to Man-Made Fibres*.

11

Dyeing

Fleeces can be obtained which have brown, fawn, grey, or almost black fibres, but the time comes when we can be more adventurous in designing threads if we dye our own colours. Dyeing can be done to the raw material or to yarn, to warp or weft yarn, to the cloth, or to the garment or article.

It is fairly difficult to obtain small quantities of some chemical dyes, although most suppliers either sell them or can put one in touch with a specialist who deals with craftsmen who wish to buy small amounts. Details are given in the *Beginner's Guide to Fabric Dyeing and Printing* in this series.

There are craftsmen who dye small amounts of raw materials or yarns for sale, and run courses. Guilds of Weavers often arrange dyeing courses.

The beginner would be well advised to start to dye with natural materials, which can be found in the garden, the fields, or the woods. Natural dyes provide a pleasing variety of colours, and they are not difficult to use.

The kitchen will provide most of the equipment which is necessary for dyeing. This includes dyebaths and a means of heating; water (soft if possible); muslin for holding dye woods; glass rods, smooth sticks, or stainless steel rods for stirring; spoons for measuring; rubber gloves; tape and oddments of yarn for identification; and a thermometer.

Natural dyestuffs

Natural dyes can be divided into two groups: substantive (non-mordant) and adjective (mordant) dyes.

Substantive dyes are very easy to use. The colour is obtained by boiling the dyestuff, and this colour, when boiled with the fibre, is fast. The majority of natural dyes need a mordant – a chemical to make the colour fast – but certain dyestuffs contain their own built-in acids.

When using natural dyes, wool is the easiest fibre with which to start. However, once a dyebath has been prepared, it is a good idea to put in a number of different fibres. In this way it will be easy to see which fibres have an affinity for a particular dyestuff (natural or chemical). Use some way of identifying the different fibres; a system of knots is useful.

Experiments will prove that wool from different breeds will give slightly different results, even though they all look alike before entering the dyebath. Try adding naturally coloured fleece too. Plain cotton, mercerised cotton, silk, linen, and synthetic materials can all be used. After blending raw materials or making mixed plies, interesting results can be obtained by using a dye which has affinity for one material and not the other.

Preparing the raw material

Wool

It is essential that the raw material should be quite clean. Scouring wool is dealt with in Chapter 4.

Wool in fleece form should have vegetable matter, seeds, or thorns removed. Lightly tease the wool apart so that the water can penetrate the mass.

When dyeing wool in yarn form, it is very important that good skeins should be prepared. Check that the skein has been tied securely and loosely.

If a tie-dyed effect is required, tie the skein tightly in places, or wrap it with polythene and tie tightly to stop the dye penetrating the yarn. If white to start with, it will come out with white patches where the threads were bound.

(a)

(b)

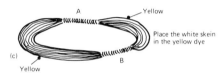

A   Yellow

Place the white skein
in the yellow dye

(c)

Yellow   B

Untie binding at B (it will be white)
Tie section C to protect yellow

A

Then place in red dye

(d)   C   B

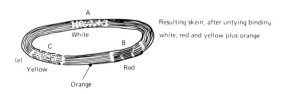

A

Resulting skein, after untying binding

White

white, red and yellow plus orange

(e)   C   B

Yellow   Red

Orange

Figure 11.1. Tie-dyeing. (a) The method. (b) The effect. (c), (d) and
(e) show stages in the production of a tie-dyed skein

Silk
If natural gum is still on silk, it should be degummed in a solution of olive oil and soap or soapflakes. Allow 1½oz of soap to 1gall of soft water. Bring the water almost to the boil and hang the silk in the liquid for 1½ hours. When the liquid has cooled, squeeze the silk gently. Repeat the process if necessary.

Manmade materials
These should only need thorough wetting-out.

Wetting-out
When textile fibres are dry, they have a natural resistance to water. All materials in whatever state must be thoroughly wetted-out before dyeing; this means that the fibres must all be wet right through to the middle. It is not sufficient to hold them under a tap or dip them in and out of a bowl of water. Place the fibre in soft warm water for a few hours; if a small amount of detergent is added, the wetting-out will be carried out more quickly.

Before dyeing, rinse and squeeze out the water. Make sure the yarn or raw material is evenly damp.

Dye liquor ratio

An important consideration is the amount of liquid required for a given amount of yarn. Beginners sometimes try to push too much material into a small pan, thus getting uneven dyeing. At least 1 pint of liquid is required for every ounce. It is advisable for beginners to use a ratio of 30:1 (i.e., 30floz to 1oz yarn. If too much liquid is used, the dye will be diluted and the colour pale.

Make sure the dyebath is large enough to hold the yarn and liquid when dyeing and mordanting. It should be possible to move the yarn around gently without the boiling liquid overflowing.

Substantive dyes

As the colour from a substantive dye is fast without the addition of extra chemicals, it is easy to start with one of these. The chief substantive dyes are obtained from many lichens and from walnuts.

Lichens
There are between 40 and 50 lichens which give dyes, including those originally used for Highland tartans and Harris tweeds.

Lichens grow on stones, rocks, walls, trees, and rooftops. They should be gathered in summer, preferably after rain,

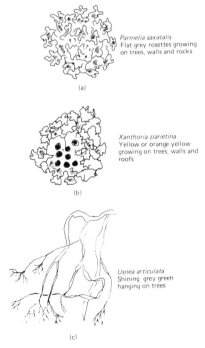

Parmelia saxatalis
Flat grey rosettes growing on trees, walls and rocks

(a)

Xanthoria parietina
Yellow or orange yellow growing on trees, walls and roofs

(b)

Usnea articulata
Shining grey green hanging on trees

(c)

Figure 11.2. Lichens

143

when they are easier to remove. They can be stored without affecting colours.

Parmelia saxatilis is found in high coastal or mountainous country on rocks, stone walls, treetrunks and roofs. It has a grey-green upper surface, and the underneath is black. Colour obtained is stone to deep red-brown according to quantity and length of time in dyebath.

Parmelia parietina or *Xanthoria parietina* grows in flat rosette shapes on walls, roofs, and rocks all over the country. It has a bright yellow-orange colour. Colour obtained is deep cream if used in its natural state, shell pink if ammonia is added, or deep dusty pink if chrome is added.

Usnea articulata is a long, grey, beard-like growth on the weather side of trees. Colour obtained is fawn to brown.

Dyeing with lichen (Method 1)

Allow 1 lb of lichen to 1 lb of wool. Put the lichen in a large pot and almost fill it with cold water.

Bring to the boil slowly, let it simmer for two to three hours and then let it get cold.

Next day, put the wool into the pot, bring to the boil, and simmer until the required depth of colour is obtained.

When the liquid is cold, remove the wool and wash it. The lichen will shake out of the wool.

— Lichen

— Wool

Figure 11.3. Dyeing with lichen (method 2)

Method 2

Put a layer of lichen at the bottom of the pot. Follow this with a layer of wool. Continue in this way until the pot is nearly full.

Fill the pot with cold water. Heat it and let it simmer for several hours.

144

This process can be repeated the next day if a darker colour is required. Remember that the colour of wet wool will look darker than when it is dry.

Colours obtained will be fast.

Walnuts
The green shell of the walnut is used for dyeing. Collect the green walnuts which fall off the tree in July and August. Cover them with water and keep from the light. An astringent colourless substance in the walnut gives a greenish-yellow dye which quickly turns dark brown after absorbing oxygen from the air.

For 1 oz of wool, use about 15 walnuts. Let the walnuts steep overnight and then simmer them in the same water. In 15 minutes, strain off the walnuts. When the liquid has cooled to hand heat, thoroughly wetted wool can be put in. It is not necessary to boil the wool very long – in fact, over-boiling would make the wool harsh.

If dyeing skeins of wool, be prepared to take them out at short intervals if a range of colours from fawn to dark brown is required: the colour is absorbed very quickly. Walnuts are used as a 'saddening' agent; that means they darken other colours. They also help to produce black.

It is possible to use the pale-brown inner shells of walnuts, but the colour is not as strong as that obtained from the husks.

Rinse the wool in hot, soft water, and squeeze it gently. Repeat this process in cooler water, then hang the wool to dry in the shade after squeezing out excess water.

Adjective dyes

Many dyes need some chemical substance to help them become permanently fixed on to the yarn. At one time it was thought that these chemicals etched or ate away the fibre so that the dyestuff could penetrate the broken-down surface. (The word 'mordant' is derived from the French verb *mordre*, to bite). A mordant is now regarded as a chemical which can

145

be fixed on the fibre and which combines with the dyestuff, forming a link which allows certain colours which have no affinity for the fibre to be fixed.

It is not difficult to use natural dyes: very little can go wrong when boiling up berries, leaves, or roots. But if mordants are not weighed exactly and used correctly, the finished results are likely to be disastrous. Good, even colours depend on thorough mordanting.

Chemicals

Alum (potassium aluminium sulphate) One of the most popular mordants, it is safe and reliable and gives clear, bright colours. These white crystals are easily obtainable from chemists. If too much alum is used, wool becomes sticky.

Chrome (potassium dichromate) Orange crystals, which should be kept in a dark jar. A pleasant mordant to use which helps to make the wool look lustrous. Too much can spoil the intended colour.

Iron (ferrous sulphate) Soft green crystals. A useful mordant for making dark colours, it needs very careful handling to prevent it from making the wool hard.

Tin (stannous chloride) Off-white crystals. This mordant has the opposite effect to iron: it brightens colours. Too much makes wool brittle.

These four chemicals are the most popular mordants in use today. Make sure that containers of chrome, iron, and tin are securely closed and labelled clearly, and keep them in a safe place.

Other useful chemicals are the following.

Cream of tartar (tartaric acid) This helps to make colours clear. It is especially valuable when producing scarlet with cochineal and tin mordant, and it is used in conjunction with iron mordant.

Salt (sodium chloride) Salt is useful to put in the dyebath to help exhaust the colour and drive it on to the fibres.

Vinegar (weak solution of acetic acid)   Useful when rinsing wool, to neutralise soap.

Glauber's salts (sodium sulphate)   They help to exhaust the dyebath.

Mordanting
One has to decide at what stage mordanting should be carried out. There are three choices: before dyeing, after dyeing, or simultaneously.

Mordanting before dyeing makes it possible to see the effect on the wool of the mordant, and it helps in deciding on the strength of colour to be prepared in the dyebath.

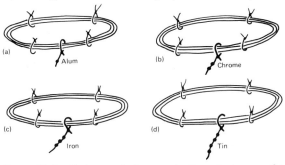

Figure 11.4.   Skeins ready for mordanting. A strong white thread with knots identifies the mordant. (a) Alum (one knot). (b) Chrome (two knots). (c) Iron (three knots). (d) Tin (four knots)

Yarns can also be mordanted and stored for future use. Make sure the skeins are labelled. Wool which has been mordanted with chrome feels soft, but wool mordanted with alum or tin has a similar appearance. Iron mordant is usually applied after dyeing for purposes of 'saddening'.

Mordanting with alum   The quantities which follow are for 1 lb of wool.

Use 4 oz alum, 1 oz cream of tartar, and 3 gall of cold soft water.

Dissolve the alum and cream of tartar in a little boiling water and add the rest of the water. Stir occasionally while the water is being heated to about 120°F (50°C).

Put in the well-wetted wool and raise the temperature to boiling point. Then let it simmer. Coarse, strong wool will need about an hour; soft, fine wool will need about three-quarters of an hour.

During mordanting, stir the wool very gently, or rather move it around gently in the simmering liquid. The liquid must evenly penetrate all parts of the skein. After the temperature has fallen, lift the wool out of the bath with a smooth rod and let it drain for a moment.

Squeeze out the excess water but do not wring or wash the wool.

The wool is ready for dyeing, but it can be left for a day or two in a linen bag, where it can stay damp.

Another way of dealing with the wool is to let it steep in the liquor all night and use it next morning after squeezing it thoroughly and evenly. If dyeing is not going to be carried out for several weeks, dry the mordanted yarn, label and store it.

Mordanting with chrome Preparations should be carried out as for alum, but it is advisable to mordant with chrome just before dyeing. Chrome is light-sensitive, so keep the vessel covered during mordanting, and after mordanting keep the yarn away from the light. Carelessness can lead to uneven dyeing.

Use ½ oz to 1 lb of wool for full shades, a little less for pale shades.

Heat the water to about 85°F (30°C). Dissolve the chrome in boiling water and add the solution to the dyebath. Put in the thoroughly wetted-out wool, making sure it is completely submerged. Cover the vessel and bring it slowly to the boil. Simmer for one hour. During this time, move the wool gently once or twice to encourage even penetration. When the wool is cool enough to handle, rinse it in warm water, squeeze it evenly, and place it in a covered vessel until the dyebath is ready.

Mordanting with tin Tin must always be used extremely carefully, as it can very easily make wool harsh and brittle.

Use ½ oz tin crystals and ½ oz cream of tartar.

Heat the water to 85°F (30°C). Dissolve the cream of tartar in boiling water and stir this into the bath. Dissolve the tin crystals in warm water and add it. Stir well. Put in the well-wetted wool and raise slowly to the boil. Simmer for an hour.

After cooling to handling temperature, rinse the wool thoroughly in warm, soapy water. Rinse again, squeeze, and then dye as soon as possible.

Rinse with soap after dyeing.

Mordanting with iron Iron is a difficult mordant to use because it can harden wool, and it can lead to uneven dyeing by attaching itself to the fibres very patchily. Try to immerse the wool quickly in order to make the liquid reach every part of the skein at the same time. Do not put it in as shown in *Figure 11.5.*

This part will absorb more
mordant than the other end

Figure 11.5. The wrong way to enter a skein, unless a special effect is required

Keep a pan specially for iron, unless stainless steel is being used. The smallest trace of iron can dull a colour.

Use ¼ to ½ oz iron and 1 oz cream of tartar.

Method of mordanting after dyeing
Dye the yarn for 45 minutes.

Dissolve the mordant in hot water and add it to the dyebath after removing the yarn and turning off the heat. Stir thoroughly, replace the yarn, raise to the boil, and simmer for 15 to 20 minutes. Move the wool around gently.

Rinse the wool very thoroughly.

Mordanting with iron after dyeing is known as 'saddening'.

If it is done carefully, the resulting colours are very attractive and have a rich underglow of colour. But it can destroy the quality of the wool, making it hard, tender, unpleasant to handle, and generally useless.

Mordanting silk The gum must be removed before mordanting (see p. 127), and then the silk washed in tepid water. Take great care with silk so that it does not lose its lustre. On the whole, silk can be mordanted like wool, but avoid high temperatures.

Mordanting cotton and linen These materials are much more difficult to dye with natural dyestuffs than are wool and silk, as their fibres are not so porous. Results are often disappointing, so on the whole it is better to use chemical dyes. However, if natural dyes are to be used, thorough mordanting must be carried out. Work with clean, scoured, bleached cotton or linen.

Collecting adjective dyestuffs
Natural dyestuffs can be obtained from leaves, flowers, fruit, roots, and bark.

As a rough guide, use 1 lb of dyestuff to 1 lb of wool. Many natural dyes give rather a pale colour, so weigh them generously.

Leaves Collect young green leaves such as nettle, bracken, and blackberry, and use them at once. Heat gently to help preserve the green colour. Some leaves from trees are harder and may need to be broken up and soaked before being used.

Berries Try to collect berries when they are over-ripe and use them at once. Crush them with a hammer if they are hard.

Bark Using barks of trees can be interesting. Carpenters and woodworkers can often help by supplying a variety of woods and bark, and bark can be collected from freshly felled trees. The best colour is usually obtained from the inner bark. Cut the bark into pieces and soak it overnight, then boil for at least two hours.

Flowers Flowers and petals should be used immediately after picking. Wallflowers are a good source of colour; in springtime they are often pulled up while there are many flowers left on them.

Other materials Do not be afraid to experiment.

Using adjective dyes

Place the plant, root, or berries in a pan of soft water and heat until the dye is extracted. If hard materials such as chips of wood are being used, soak these overnight and use the same water for boiling the dyestuff. They can be tied loosely in muslin to make their removal easier.

Strain the liquid and discard the plants, etc. Cool the liquid to hand heat and then put in the clean, thoroughly wetted-out material.

Heat the liquid until it simmers, then leave the yarn in the pan until the desired colour is obtained. Remember that wet colour usually looks darker than a dry one. While the yarn is being dyed, move it gently from time to time so that the colour can penetrate the fibres evenly. Do not let it rise above the level of the liquid.

When satisfied with the colour, lift out the skein on a smooth rod and let it drip for a short while.

Rinse the skein several times, starting with hot water and getting progressively cooler.

Squeeze the wool to remove excess liquid. The skeins can be placed in a bag or pillowcase and spun in a spin dryer, or they can be hung in the open air, out of direct sunlight, to dry.

Onion skins To obtain different shades of yellow, orange, and brown from onion skins, take four skeins of wool, weigh them when dry, and mordant the skeins with alum, chrome, iron, and tin respectively. Remember to tie knots to identify the mordants used. Prepare the dyebath by boiling onion skins in soft water. The colour will quickly run from the skins and a beautiful golden liquid will appear. Strain the liquid and let it cool before placing the damp mordanted wool in it.

Bought natural dyestuffs

Some natural dyestuffs can be bought from suppliers. These can be used for stronger colours, as British plants can sometimes be rather disappointing. The principal ones are logwood chips, fustic chips, cochineal, and madder.

Follow the general instructions for mordanting and dyeing when using these materials. For 1 lb of wool, use the following quantities.

Logwood chips   2 oz for purple, blue, black.

Fustic chips   6 oz for golden yellow, olive.

Ground cochineal   1 oz for scarlet, crimson, purple.

Madder   4 oz to 6 oz for vermilion, pink.

Indigo

Although it is a natural dye, indigo requires special treatment in order to obtain the colour. It can be used on wool, but it is safer when used to dye cotton. The caustic soda involved can be harmful to wool, so great care must be taken over weights.

The dyestuff is not soluble in water, so a stock solution has to be made using sodium dithionite (sodium hydrosulphite) and caustic soda. Some recipes are very complicated, but the following one has been simplified. A 7 lb stone jamjar and a teaspoon are used.

Fill the jamjar one-third full of water at 120°F (50°C) – i.e. hand-hot. Stir in one teaspoon of caustic soda followed by one teaspoon of sodium dithionite. Next add from one to three teaspoons of indigo powder. If the jamjar is held between the hands and gently shaken round, the indigo will become dissolved. It is important to avoid getting oxygen into the mixture.

Add hand-hot water to the jar until it is two-thirds full. Give the contents another swish by gently turning the jar between the hands.

Let the mixture stand for 10 minutes. It will appear to be a greenish-yellow colour.

Enter the well-boiled and wetted-out cotton; try to avoid making bubbles. Leave the cotton in the jar for about 15 minutes.

Lift the skein out of the liquid and let it hang in the air. At first it appears yellow, then green, and finally a permanent blue. (De-oxidised indigo is yellow, and as it takes oxygen from the air, it becomes blue.)

In order to get darker colours, build up the shade by dipping repeatedly. Always allow the yarn to stay in the air for the same length of time as it has been dipped. Although the dyebath is getting colder, it can go on being used.

Before drying the cotton, rinse the skeins in hot water and one tablespoon of acetic acid; rinse in very hot soapy water, and then rinse in clear water until there is no loose dye.

Woad

Woad is another ancient dye used for blue. Woad plants grow in various parts of England, but it can be fairly difficult to obtain blue from the leaves unless they are picked at the right time. Dr David Hill of Bristol University has provided the following successful recipe.

Pick the leaves of the plants before they start to flower – in the first year if sown in spring. Break them up and drop them in boiling water for one to three minutes. Strain the leaves off and discard them. Cool the pale greenish yellow liquid and then add a few drops of ammonia, enough to make the liquid go dark yellow or green.

Aerate the liquid for a considerable time until it has gone as dark a green as it seems likely to go. Re-heat it to scalding but not boiling temperature, adding a saltspoon or coffeespoon of sodium dithionite per quart.

Leave the liquid until it goes clear with whitish coagulated lumps in it.

Add the yarn, and from then on, treat as for indigo.

12

Designing

While learning the skill which enables us to practise the craft of spinning, we must always be aware of the design possibilities which are developing in front of our eyes. The beauty of threads is not sufficiently appreciated; how can we make the most of their visual possibilities?

We need to be aware of the sources of inspiration around us. We can see examples of craftwork in museums and we can visit exhibitions and see what our contemporaries are doing. There are many ways in which we can help to train our eyes to be visually aware of our environment. It is helpful to draw and paint from nature to train the eye to see the development of shape, proportion, texture, colour, and rhythm. Pencil, pen, paint, paper, threads, cloth, and many other materials can all be used to assist this practical work.

Getting to know fleece

Having practised a number of techniques, it should be possible to be more selective. Try to see what a fleece will let you do, and discover which type of yarn is likely to be the best one to spin from those fibres. At first, let the fleece be the guide – do not try to force it into an uncharacteristic yarn.

Prepare the fibres by a method of your choice. Spin a sufficient length of each type so that it can be washed and inspected before the decision is made concerning the yarn to be spun.

Is it possible to make yarns that are very fine, very thick, tightly twisted or loosely twisted, all from the same fleece? The answer will depend on many factors: for example, the breed of sheep and the part of the fleece which has been chosen, the preparation of the fibres, the equipment being used, and the skill of the spinner.

After experimenting, make skeins of the yarn, tie them, wash them, and then examine them carefully. It should then be possible to come to a conclusion as to the best method of spinning that fleece for a particular purpose.

Never throw away any spun threads – failures one day can be just what is wanted on another occasion.

Z and S twist in design

As already explained, the direction of twist has a great influence on the design of the yarn and on the resulting cloth. It is particularly useful to consider the twists when producing a crepe material.

Sometimes when very fine threads are used with alternate Z and S twists, one of the threads can be tinted in order to distinguish one from the other. Washing removes the colour and the cloth then shows its distinctive pattern.

If a travelling rug has been woven from Z-twisted singles yarn, the fringe can be made by giving the threads an extra twist and letting them form the opposite twist when held together. The fringe must be made before washing.

Blending colours

There are many ways of introducing colour into spinning. One of the most satisfying is to blend dyed fleece. Colours can be blended in a fairly random way, or they can be carded so carefully that individual colours disappear. Beware of using too many colours at the same time.

The following suggestions are for using black and white, as they will give good contrast. Start by teasing the fleeces and placing them in two piles. Spin a yarn by taking fibres from each pile alternately. This will result in a black and white yarn with a mixture between.

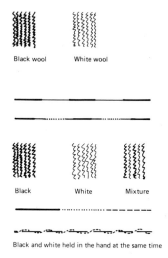

Black wool

White wool

Black

White

Mixture

Black and white held in the hand at the same time

Figure 12.1. Using teased wool to make blended yarn

This method is useful for Navaho plying (p. 165). The yarn could be spun with equal lengths of colour, or there could be a regular pattern of long and short colour sequences.

Blending in a planned proportion

Arrange piles of wool as described below and mix each together with the fingers. This will result in rough-and-ready shading; a more exact effect would be obtained by careful carding.

Start with 10 parts of black and 10 parts of white fleece. Take nine parts black and one part white, then eight parts black and two parts white, then seven parts black and three parts white, and so on. Continue in this way until the black has been completely worked out and the thread is all white.

By spinning in this way, it is possible to spin lengths shaded from solid black to solid white. On a larger scale, one could make skeins of yarn in each shade.

This type of blending can be carried out in many other ways, using colours of one's own choice. E.g. take a strong colour and add various amounts of white, or darken it by gradually adding more black. Unusual and unexpected results can be obtained by blending other pairs of colours. Do not be afraid to experiment, for small lengths can be tried first. There are safe colour schemes, such as black and white plus one strong colour, or different shades of colours given by one dye used with different mordants: e.g. bright yellow, gold, olive, and orange from onion skins.

Try blending pairs of colours while working round the colour circle: red and orange, orange and yellow, yellow and green, green and blue, blue and indigo, indigo and purple, and purple and red.

Blending on carders

Blending by teasing only can be haphazard, and a large amount of more evenly blended yarn may be required. If very controlled blending is suitable, amounts can be weighed exactly.

The ideas suggested above can be carried out with carders, but the kind of blends will depend on the thoroughness of blending.

Colours can be blended together so carefully that it is impossible to tell which were used in the first place. This is necessary for a suiting or dress material where a flat overall colour is required. A blob of colour appearing on the surface would be a mistake in this sort of material, whereas blobs of colour arranged in a rhythmical way would clearly be there on purpose to add colour or textural interest.

The designer has to decide on the type of blend required. This involves choosing the method of carding, the shade of the finished cloth, and deciding whether the colours are to be blended so carefully that it is impossible to see the original colours.

Carding can be carried out in any of the following ways.

1. Place a thin layer of one colour across the carder and then cover it with a layer of the second colour. Repeat this until

there is enough for a rolag. Brush and card these colours until they are sufficiently blended.

2. Card thin layers of colour separately and then place them together for the final rolling into the rolag.

3. For coloured stripes, use two colours and arrange them in stripes on the carders. Work with an odd number of stripes: i.e. three, five, or seven (*Figure 12.2*).

Two sets of rolags should be made for each colour scheme.

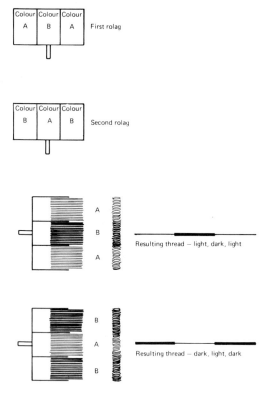

Figure 12.2. Blending with carders. (a) Three stripes to each rolag.

158

If the carder is going to be divided into three sections, make half the rolags with colour A on the outside and colour B on the inside. For the other rolags, place colour B on the outside and colour A in the middle. When spinning, use rolag 1 followed by rolag 2 for a regular colour arrangement. The thread will have a dip-dyed effect, and between each colour there will be a blended area.

Many other ways of combining colours can be used.

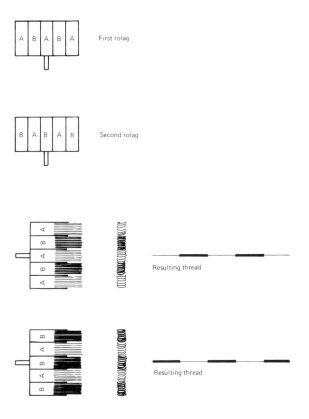

First rolag

Second rolag

Resulting thread

Resulting thread

(b) Five stripes to each rolag

159

Adding coloured knops (neps)
Little spots of colour can be added during carding. After the last brushing, drop small balls of coloured wool over the carded wool and pat them down with the back of the carder.

Blending mixed fibres before dyeing
Very interesting results can be obtained by blending fibres before dyeing and then putting the skeins into different types of dyestuff.

Plying

Plying is also known as doubling or folding. This is easy to understand if one holds a fairly tightly twisted yarn and lets the tension slacken: loops fold back on themselves or become doubled.

Yarn is plied in order to give it strength, to change the way it handles, to change its colour, to introduce other materials, or to make it thicker.

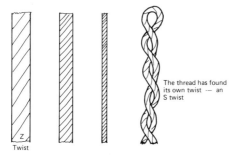

Twist

Add extra twist

The thread has found its own twist — an S twist

Figure 12.3. Folding yarn for plying

Worsted threads are usually plied; woollen yarns can be used singly or plied. Knitting wools are usually plied.

When a singles yarn is plied in the reverse twist, some of the original twist will be lost. If a tightly spun thread with a Z twist has extra twist added, and is folded in half and then

160

allowed to twist on itself, it will form an S twist. If too much twist has travelled up a short length of wool during spinning, when the tension is released, the yarn will twist on itself, making 'snarls'.

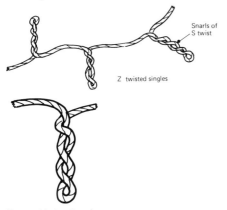

Figure 12.4. Snarls

Yarns can be plied on the spindle or wheel. The advantage of using a spindle is that really thick, bulky threads can be plied, whereas with a wheel this is possible only with a large orifice.

Preparing spools
Use a bobbin winder and cut out oval shapes of paper for spools; or use old cardboard spools, packed with tissue paper if they are too large.

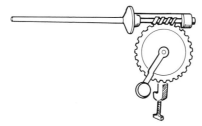

Figure 12.5. A bobbin winder

Balls of wool can be wound so that the beginning and the end can be drawn off at the same time. A yarn winder, as used by machine knitters, is useful for this purpose.

Spool racks can be bought from suppliers in a great variety of shapes and sizes, but simple ones can easily be made from cardboard boxes and knitting needles.

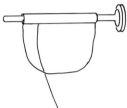

Figure 12.6. Making spools from paper

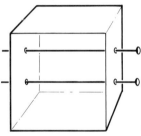

Figure 12.7. Spool rack made from cardboard box and knitting needles

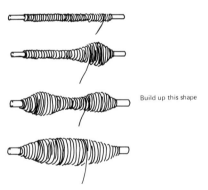

Build up this shape

Figure 12.8. Winding a bobbin

Making two-ply with the spindle

Two bobbins taken from the spinning-wheel would be ready at once for plying. Try to have about the same amount on each bobbin by spinning the same number of rolags, or equal weights of wool, on each. Separate spools can be wound and placed on a lazy kate or in a home-made box.

If using a suspended spindle, tie the two handspun ends to the spindle shaft and then hitch them round the tip of the spindle.

The two threads should be held each side of the middle finger, about 12 in away from the tip of the spindle.

Twist the spindle anticlockwise, putting in an S twist. When sufficient twist has travelled up, slide the left hand along another 12 in and ply that length. Make sure each thread is coming through the fingers evenly. If one singles is tighter than the other, there will be an uneven twist (*Figure 12.9*).

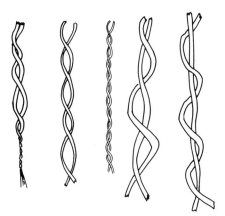

Figure 12.9. Uneven plying

Wind the two-ply on to the spindle, and when the stem is full make a skein and tie it in the usual way.

There is no limit to the number of ends which can be plied together on the spindle. Obviously, the size of each singles will determine the eventual thickness.

Plying on the spinning-wheel
Place the bobbins on a spool rack.

Increase the tension on the driving-band.

Tie the two handspun ends to the starter yarn, or thread them through the orifice and tie them to the bobbin.

Hold the two yarns in the right hand with one yarn at each side of the first finger. Keep the yarn taut between the orifice and the right hand.

Spin the wheel in an anti-clockwise direction (if using Z-twisted yarn) and treadle rhythmically.

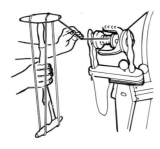

Figure 12.10. Skeining, using a niddy-noddy

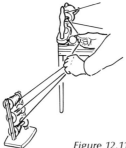

Figure 12.11. Plying three yarns

Watch the amount of twist being put into the yarn and stop after a while to examine the yarn. Move the yarn along the bobbin by using the guide hooks in turn. The two-ply will build up fairly quickly.

164

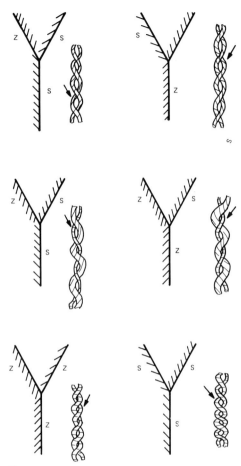

Figure 12.12. Mixing twists

Navaho plying

The Navaho method is a very useful one because it is a way of making a type of three-ply yarn from a singles thread without having to wind three separate bobbins. The singles thread is made into large loops, rather as in making a chain stitch in crochet, or chaining a warp. The loops measure about 8in.

The looped end is fastened to the starter yarn and the wheel is turned to the left or right, depending on the required twist. As the wool is plied and wound on to the bobbin, more large loops have to be formed. This method is useful for making a thick thread in blocks of colour.

The Navaho method can be used to ply a singles thread spun in known lengths of alternate colours.

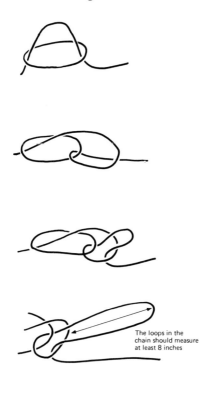

The loops in the chain should measure at least 8 inches

Figure 12.13. Navaho plying

166

Fancy-spun threads

Fancy-spun yarns serve a useful purpose in decorating and adding character to a cloth. They are very good for weaving tapestries, decorative hangings, and furnishings.

A successful fancy-spun yarn depends on construction and on colour: the construction may be extremely clever, but if the overall effect is dull and uninteresting, the yarn is not likely to be successful. A fancy yarn is usually added as decoration to a fabric, and the special effect will probably be modified and subdued when woven. So that it will enhance the material and not get lost in the weave, bear in mind the design of the cloth when designing such a yarn. Vivid colour combinations are possible, but try to picture their effect from a distance.

Fancy yarns are more expensive to buy because of the extra time taken to produce them, but a hand-spinner can make just the required lengths in a variety of colours and materials.

Plying and design
The choice of yarns for plying will have an important effect on the resulting threads. This choice can include yarns which are thick and thin; tightly or loosely twisted; Z-twisted or S-twisted; lustrous or non-lustrous; coloured; slubbed; or made from mixed fibres.

Mixed colours can look very attractive or they can look as if they are having a war with each other. If two singles of equal intensity and brightness are plied together, they can spoil each other.

Designing fancy-spun yarns
Fancy-spun yarns can be produced in three main ways.

In the preparation of the fibre   This is done by mixing fibres while carding, or by adding coloured knops (compact balls of fibre).

In the spinning   Such yarns include slub yarns, which have tightly twisted thin places and thick lumps of unspun fibre,

167

arranged regularly or irregularly; yarns with different thicknesses made by drafting irregular amounts; irregular twisting with variety in turns per inch; and coloured effects made by spinning with two rovings in one hand.

Figure 12.14. Slub yarns

In twisting   The effect of twisting can lead to corkscrew or bead threads; excess delivery can produce gimp, bouclé, cover, snarl, loop, and irregular-spot threads; intermittent delivery can add yet more variety.

Some suggestions for experimenting
Take a slub yarn and a binder (a fine thread). When plying, twist slub yarn and binder in the same direction; or insert the twist in the opposite direction; or hold the slub yarn tightly and let the binder wind loosely; or insert twist in the same direction and then add another binder in the opposite direction.

Take two slub yarns. Make two-ply with slubs coinciding; or with slubs alternating.

Take thick and thin threads and vary the delivery rate. Let the thick thread spiral round the thin one by delivering it at a slightly quicker speed, making a gimp; or allow the thick thread to be delivered much more quickly and then bind this thread with a very fine one in the opposite direction.

Make cover yarns by taking two yarns and controlling them separately so that they cover each other alternately. They can cover each other in many ways, and they can be allowed to twist backwards and forwards, making knots.

Snarl yarn is made with a highly twisted effect yarn used with a core yarn. The effect yarn is delivered in a very slack way so that it forms a continuous series of snarls. This should then be bound in the reverse direction with a fine thread to hold the snarls in position.

Fancy-spun yarns should be skeined, washed, and stretched before being used.

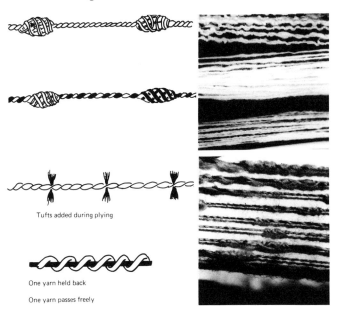

Tufts added during plying

One yarn held back

One yarn passes freely

Figure 12.15. Fancy-spun threads

Using Jacob fleece

The Jacob sheep is a very popular breed with hand-spinners. In one fleece there is often great variety, ranging from fine, soft wool, to coarse, rough wool. Colour varies a great deal: it can be white, grey, light brown, or dark brown, and a hand-spinner is in a position to appreciate the variety, which in a factory will cause problems.

A Jacob fleece should be white with well-defined spots or dark patches. The wool should be of fine quality and not kempy.

Preparing a Jacob fleece

Unroll the fleece (see Chapter 2). Carefully spread it out and examine the distribution of the coloured wool: the amount of each colour will help to decide the design. Some fleeces will be mostly white with a small amount of brown, others will have equal quantities, while some fleeces are almost all brown.

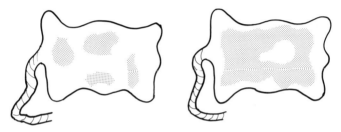

Figure 12.16. Distribution of brown and white in Jacob fleeces

The fleece can be sorted in two ways: according to quality of wool regardless of colour; or according to quality and colour. Some spinners use the colours at random, which can give the overall effect seen on the sheep.

Uses

If the fleece is a fairly coarse one, it may be more suitable for floor rugs than anything else. Slightly twisted rolags can be used on a linen or cotton warp. The colours can be blended in many ways, or they can be taken separately. Slightly twisted fleece can be used to make pile by tying knots into the warp.

Single or plied wool can be used for jackets, dresses, and scarves if the fleece is of a very soft type. The finished article should be visualised so that the yarn can be suitably designed. Small squares can be made and joined together (a good way of using up experimental skeins).

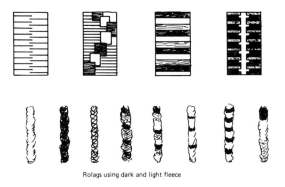

Rolags using dark and light fleece

Figure 12.17. Rolags made from dark and light Jacob fleece

Figure 12.18. Spin and knit, working on two sleeves alternately

Figure 12.19. Lampshades using alternate colours, shading or fancy-spun yarns

More ambitious spinners might like to try a large bulky knitted coat. Yarns can be spun to order as the work progresses.

If a coat or jumper is to be made in a symmetrical pattern, it is advisable to start several pieces at the same time and let the pattern develop gradually. This will avoid getting to the last sleeve and discovering that there is not enough wool left of a particular colour or quality.

171

Jumpers in patchwork designs could be knitted. If a little colour is also added, the natural colours of the Jacob fleece would form a very attractive background for a small amount of bright yarn.

Most of the suggestions given for knitting could be carried out in crochet. Granny-squares joined together, or raised patterns on cushion covers, would also be possible. Pictures to hang on the wall could be made by any of the techniques described, mixing different shades and thicknesses of yarn. If a lampshade frame is filled with threads, it can look very attractive.

13

Knitting

These questions should be considered when knitting with handspun wool.

How much clean yarn can be obtained from a fleece? After sorting, selecting, washing, and spinning, it is possible to

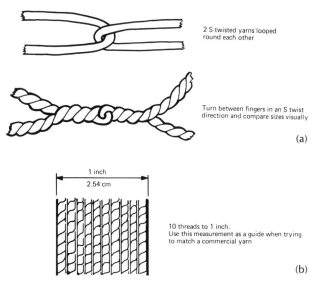

2 S-twisted yarns looped round each other

Turn between fingers in an S twist direction and compare sizes visually

(a)

10 threads to 1 inch.
Use this measurement as a guide when trying to match a commercial yarn

(b)

Figure 13.1. Checking size of yarn. (a) By comparison with commercial yarn. (b) By measurement

lose up to 50 per cent of the original dirty, greasy wool. This is important if it is intended to knit a garment entirely from one particular fleece, such as a Jacob.

How does one estimate quantities and size of yarn to be spun? Samples should always be knitted to check tension, measurements, and size of needles. If comparing handspun wool with commerically spun yarns loop one in the other and twist. Compare the two thicknesses by eye.

To match a commercial yarn, wind a sample of it round a ruler and check the number of threads required for 1 in. Then try to reproduce this thickness by spinning sample lengths and winding them round the ruler.

Should yarn be plied? It is safer to ply the yarn before knitting as the garment will lie flat. But singles can be used successfully if the following hints are followed.

After skeining, keep yarns under tension before and after washing; start knitting from the end of the yarn which was spun first; knit a lacy pattern or knit two rows of S twist and two rows of Z twist alternately.

14

Spinning today

Most people spin by hand for pleasure or for the satisfaction of being able to design their own yarns and see a project through from the raw material to the finished article. A few people are able to make a profit from their activities. There is a spinner in Victoria, Australia, who made enough money to pay her return fare to England, and a New Zealand spinner made enough money to buy a racehorse.

Because spinning can be so time-consuming, it is probably advantageous to spin luxury threads which can be used sparingly. However, there are some dedicated spinners who spin all their own threads for both warp and weft, and make long lengths of cloth, either for furnishings or clothes.

Arthur Haynes described in the June 1975 issue of the London Guild's journal *Warp and Weft* how he worked out the time taken to spin a 7lb fleece. This is his timetable.

	Hours	Min
Unroll and sort into five grades	1	00
Tease and card (1½oz per hour)	74	40
Spin (3oz per hour)	37	20
Skein (3oz skeins, 5 min each)	3	05
Scour (enter, rinse, dry, twist up)	3	00
Total	119	05

Losses in fleece weight reduced the 7lb to 4lb 10oz.

However, spinning brings rewards which cannot be bought with money.

Spinning in education

Several schools have introduced spinning, dyeing, and weaving into their curriculum. One such school in Pontefract, West Yorkshire, has been running an examination course in these subjects since 1947.

It is possible to specialise in hand-spinning in some art colleges, polytechnics, and universities.

A number of further education establishments run excellent courses in spinning. Local authorities and libraries can often give the necessary information.

Guilds of spinners

Guilds of spinners, dyers, and weavers make an extremely valuable contribution to the textile crafts. Enthusiastic members give up a great deal of time to organise meetings, seminars, summer schools, and weekend courses. In Britain, the number of guilds has increased rapidly and they have been responsible for giving many spinners encouragement and practical assistance.

The Handweavers' Guild of America was started in the summer of 1969 by a handful of spinners, weavers, and dyers. Its magazine, *Shuttle, Spindle and Dyepot*, first published in December 1969, has grown from 18 pages to almost 100 today.

There is great enthusiasm for spinning, dyeing, and weaving guilds in Australia. Guilds also flourish in New Zealand, Canada, and South Africa.

Appendix 1

Suppliers

British Wool Marketing Board, Oak Mills, Station Rd, Clayton, Bradford, West Yorks.
Fleece.

Campden Weavers, 16 Lower High St, Chipping Campden, Glos, GL55 6DY
Quarterly booklet *Loomcraft*, books, equipment.

Colour Craft (Elizabeth Lewis), 37 Woodlands Way, Tarporley, Cheshire
Dyes, chemicals and utensils.

Craftsman's Mark Ltd, Tone Dale Mill, Wellington, Somerset TA21 0AW
Fleece, sisal, jute, flax.

K. R. Drummond, 30 Hart Grove, Ealing Common, London W5 3NB
Books.

Dryad, PO Box 38, Northgates, Leicester, LE1 9BU
Books, equipment.

Susan Foster's Weaving Studio, 9 Windermere Rd, Kendal, Cumbria
Equipment, fleece, books.

Haldane & Co. (Woodturners) Ltd, Dept. WJ, Gateside, Fife, KY 7ST
Manufacturer of Hebridean and Shetland wheels. Distributor of Ashford wheels and looms, Louët wheels and drum carders.

Jamieson & Smith (Shetland Wool Brokers) Ltd, SF Dept 90 North Rd, Lerwick, Shetland
Real Shetland fleece in white, black, moorit, and grey.

Handweavers' Studio, 29 Haroldstone Rd, London E17 7AN
Wheels, materials, equipment, books, tuition.

Frank Herring & Sons, 27 High West St, Dorchester, Dorset
  Wheels, accessories.
Kineton Gallery, Banbury St, Kineton, Warwicks
  Wheels, equipment, books, tuition.
London Textile Workshop, 65 Roseberry Rd, London N10 2LE
  Natural and synthetic dyes, mordants, chemicals, tuition.
Spinners Choice Textile Workshop and Gallery, 7 Johnston Terrace, Edinburgh
  Mail order.
Textile Bookshop (Andrea Jeavons), Tynwald Mills, St. Johns, Isle of Man
  Books and magazines on textiles.
Tynsell Handspinners (Joan Lawler), 3 Chapel Brow, Tintwistle near Hyde, Cheshire
  Spinning equipment and fibres.
The Yarn Store, 89A Grosvenor Ave, Highbury, London N5 2NL
  Equipment, materials, yarns, tuition.

Appendix 2

Bibliography

Baines, Patricia	*Spinning-wheels*	Batsford
	British Sheep Breeds	British Wool Marketing Board
Chadwick, Eileen	*The Craft of Handspinning*	Batsford
Cook, J. G.	*Handbook of Textile Fibres*	Merrow
Crockett, Candace	*The Complete Spinning Book*	Watson-Guptill
Davenport, Elsie	*Your Handspinning*	Craft & Hobby Book Service, California
Duncan, Molly	*Spin Your Own Wool*	Reed
Fannin, Allen	*Handspinning*	Van Nostrand Reinhold
	Textile Machinery	HM Stationery Office
Klein, Bernat	*Eye for Colour*	Klein with Collins
Leadbeater, Eliza	*Handspinning*	Studio Vista
Ponting, Kenneth	*Sheep of the World*	Blandford Press
Robertson, Seonaid	*Dyes from Plants*	Van Nostrand Reinhold
Teal, Peter	*Hand Wool Combing and Spinning*	Blandford Press

Journals

The Quarterly Journal	published by the Association of Handweavers' Guilds in Britain
Shuttle, Spindle and Dyepot	published by the Handweavers' Guild of America
The Web	a New Zealand publication
Crafts Magazine	published by the Crafts Council of Great Britain

Index

182